2025 EDITION

AI

ADVANCED

CODING

ADAPTABLE

STRUCTURES

Building Scalable, Intelligent, and Self-Optimizing Systems

DR. JIM LEWIS

2025 EDITON

AI Advanced

Coding

Adaptable

Structures

Building Scalable, Intelligent, and Self-Optimizing
Systems.

Dr. Jim Lewis

Disclaimer:

All trademarks, registered trademarks, and brand names mentioned in this book are the property of their respective owners. This book is an independent work and is not affiliated with, endorsed by, or sponsored by any trademark holders. The use of these names is for informational and educational purposes only and does not imply any association with the trademark owners.

Table of Contents

Introduction.

Artificial intelligence has progressed beyond static algorithms and predetermined models. The future of AI resides on adaptable structures— systems that can change, optimize, and respond to new data, settings, and obstacles without human intervention. In today's environment, when real-time decision-making is important, AI must be both scalable and self-optimizing to be effective.

The demand for adaptive AI is expanding in practically every business. Autonomous vehicles must respond to unforeseen road conditions. Fraud detection models in banking need to understand new threats as they emerge. Personalized healthcare AI systems must continuously modify their recommendations based on a patient's evolving health data. These applications require AI systems that are not just clever but also versatile and self-improving.

This book focuses on designing AI systems that adapt, learn, and scale efficiently. It is created for engineers, academics, and decision-makers who want to move beyond inflexible AI models and develop solutions that can change over time. Whether you are creating deep learning architectures, optimizing algorithms for performance, or integrating AI into large-scale applications, this book covers the necessary tools and approaches.

The Shift toward Adaptive AI.

Traditional AI models are trained on static information and often suffer when conditions change. For example, during the COVID-19 epidemic, supply chain forecasting algorithms trained on historical data failed to predict the interruptions created by lockdowns and changed customer behavior. Companies that depended on rigid AI models experienced serious forecasting errors, while those that employed adaptive AI systems—which could absorb real-time data and alter their projections accordingly—were able to respond effectively.

The same approach applies to cybersecurity. Attackers constantly create new approaches, and static security models quickly become old. Adaptive AI, on the other hand, may identify emerging dangers by evaluating behavioral patterns in real-time and modifying its detection algorithms accordingly.

The drive toward adaptable AI is not just a trend—it is a necessity in a world where data is continuously changing. AI systems must be built to learn continuously, optimize themselves, and scale seamlessly without requiring frequent retraining.

Why Adaptability Matters in AI Engineering.

Building adaptive AI involves more than just training better models. It entails building modular systems, scalable infrastructures, and self-improving algorithms that can work efficiently under changing situations.

Several essential elements describe flexible AI engineering:

1. Modularity and Scalability.

AI systems should be developed in a modular approach, allowing separate components to be updated, changed, or enhanced without affecting the entire system. For example, large-scale recommendation algorithms, like those used by Netflix and YouTube, are built on micro services. Each component—content filtering, user activity analysis, and ranking algorithms—can be updated separately, ensuring continual improvement without affecting the entire platform.

2. Real-Time Learning and Continuous Optimization.

Static models grow outdated rapidly. Modern AI must learn in real-time, responding to new inputs without requiring frequent retraining. For example, self-driving cars rely on reinforcement learning to modify their driving patterns based on road conditions. They learn from every excursion, enhancing their ability to navigate varied terrains and weather situations.

3. Hybrid Intelligence: Combining Rule-Based and Learning-Based Approaches.

Many firms struggle with AI models that lack explainability. A totally data-driven model may give highly accurate outcomes, but without apparent explanation. By merging rule-based systems with machine learning, AI may deliver both accuracy and interpretability. This is particularly useful in fields like healthcare diagnostics, where clinicians need to understand why an AI system made a particular decision.

4. Automated Hyperparameter Tuning and Meta-Learning.

AI engineers spend significant time fine-tuning models to reach optimal performance. With meta-learning, AI systems can learn how to optimize themselves, reducing human intervention. Companies like Google and OpenAI employ AutoML (Automated Machine Learning) to dynamically alter model parameters and topologies based on evolving data.

Challenges in Building Adaptable AI.

Despite the benefits, developing flexible AI is not without its problems. Some of the main obstacles include:

Computational Costs: Real-time learning and adaptability demand tremendous computational resources. Training and deploying AI models that continuously evolve can be expensive.

Data Privacy and Security: Adaptive AI systems rely on ongoing data collecting, which creates worries regarding user privacy and compliance with rules like GDPR and CCPA.

Model Drift: AI models might worsen over time if they learn from biased or incomplete data. Without sufficient monitoring, they may perpetuate undesired tendencies instead of increasing performance.

Ethical and Regulatory Concerns: Self-improving AI can produce unexpected consequences. For example, an adaptive AI trading system that learns how to maximize profits can exploit gaps in financial markets, leading to unethical behavior.

Developers must account for these problems when creating AI architectures that prioritize accountability, fairness, and security.

Real-World Applications of Adaptable AI.

The power of adaptive AI is already impacting businesses globally. Here are a few instances of how businesses and scholars are utilizing these concepts today:

Retail & E-Commerce: Amazon's AI-powered recommendation system constantly refines itself based on customer interactions. Instead of depending on a static model, it regularly modifies its algorithms to improve product recommendations.

Finance & Fraud Detection: Mastercard utilizes AI that adapts to new fraud trends in real-time, helping detect fraudulent transactions that traditional rule-based systems could overlook.

Healthcare & Personalized Medicine: AI-driven diagnostics, like IBM Watson Health, change their models depending on fresh medical research and patient data, allowing doctors to acquire the newest insights tailored to particular patients.

Autonomous Systems: Tesla's Full Self-Driving (FSD) system relies on real-time learning from millions of vehicles on the road, continuously improving its ability to handle unpredictable driving scenarios.

These applications underscore the growing need for AI that can learn, adapt, and make judgments in dynamic contexts.

What to Expect in This Book.

This book gives a realistic and organized approach to developing AI systems that are scalable, flexible, and self-optimizing. Each chapter covers critical aspects of AI engineering, from advanced neural network architectures to continuous learning frameworks.

Chapter 1 lays the foundation for adaptable AI, discussing the core principles and engineering challenges.

Chapter 2 focuses on sophisticated machine learning architectures, including transformers and hybrid AI models.

Chapter 3 addresses optimization methodologies, including reinforcement learning, AutoML, and meta-learning.

Chapter 4 provides insights into scalable AI engineering, covering cloud-based deployments, micro services, and CI/CD pipelines for AI.

Chapter 5 addresses ethical, regulatory, and security concerns in AI adaptability, ensuring responsible development and deployment.

By the end of this book, you will have a comprehensive understanding of how to construct AI systems that are not just powerful but also flexible and robust. The goal is to transcend beyond standard AI development and create intelligent systems that can evolve alongside the world they work in.

AI is no longer simply about accuracy and efficiency—it is about flexibility and resilience. In a world of continuously moving data, economic shifts, and developing user behavior, AI must be designed to learn, optimize, and scale effortlessly.

Building adaptive AI is a challenging yet rewarding challenge. The future belongs to AI systems that do not merely execute specified tasks but actively shape and refine themselves to meet the needs of the environment around them. Let us build that future—one adaptive structure at a time.

Chapter 1: Foundations of AI Adaptable Coding.

1.1 Understanding Adaptability in AI Systems.

Artificial intelligence is no longer about constructing models that follow rigorous instructions. The world moves too fast for static AI systems to remain helpful for long. Businesses, researchers, and developers increasingly focus on AI that can adapt to changing circumstances, optimize itself, and work well without frequent human intervention.

Adaptable AI is vital in many industries. Financial fraud detection systems must recognize new attack patterns in real time. Autonomous vehicles need to respond to unexpected road conditions. Customer service chatbots must enhance their responses as they interact with users. Without adaptability, AI systems quickly become obsolete.

This chapter breaks down what adaptability means in AI, why it matters, and how to create AI systems that can evolve over time.

What Makes an AI System Adaptable?

An AI system is adaptable when it can adjust its behavior, increase performance, or modify its outputs based on new data or external variables. This is distinct from standard AI models that require constant retraining by engineers.

Adaptability in AI can be measured by:

a. 1. How well it responds to new data without retraining.

2. How successfully it optimizes itself over time.

3. How seamlessly it incorporates changes without affecting previous functionality.

A notable illustration of adaptation is Google's search algorithm. Every day, individuals search for things in ways that have never been typed before. Instead of breaking, Google's AI automatically upgrades itself, learning from user interactions to better search rankings.

Another example is Tesla's Full Self-Driving (FSD) technology. Unlike typical cars, Tesla vehicles constantly receive new software updates that boost their autonomous capabilities. Every mile driven by Tesla cars contributes to a common learning system, making the AI better for all vehicles.

These systems are designed to learn continually, change in real time, and enhance efficiency without human intervention.

Types of Adaptability in AI

Not all AI systems adapt in the same way. Some update their models in real time, while others adjust their strategy based on external feedback. There are three primary types of adaptability in AI:

1. Continuous Learning AI.

This sort of AI updates itself as it receives fresh data. It does not wait for engineers to retrain it—it improves itself dynamically.

Example: Spotify's recommendation system. The more a user listens to music, the better Spotify recognizes their taste. Instead of depending on outdated data, the algorithm updates instantaneously after every encounter.

How it works: These AI models utilize reinforcement learning or online learning approaches to alter predictions on the fly.

2. Context-Aware AI.

Some AI models do not change their basic structure, but they adjust their answers depending on the situation they work in.

Example: Apple's Siri and Google Assistant. If you ask about the weather at home versus while abroad, the AI delivers different responses based on location data.

How it works: These systems employ external signals (such as GPS, user preferences, or recent interactions) to adjust their outputs dynamically.

3. Self-Optimizing AI.

These AI systems increase their performance over time by altering their own internal mechanisms. They optimize their parameters without needing human involvement.

Example: Google's AlphaGo. The AI played millions of Go games against itself, adapting its approach to beat human world champions.

How it works: Self-optimizing AI relies on approaches like meta-learning, automated hyperparameter tuning, and evolutionary algorithms to optimize its own performance.

Each of these approaches contributes to making AI systems more flexible to real-world settings.

Why Adaptability Matters More Than Ever.

AI systems that fail to adapt become worthless over time. In industries that develop swiftly, the ability to respond determines whether AI provides value or creates problems.

1. Businesses Rely on AI to Keep Up with Fast-Changing Markets.

E-commerce enterprises utilize AI-driven inventory management systems to estimate demand. If these models are not adaptive, they may hoard the wrong things, leading to losses.

Example: During the COVID-19 outbreak, AI demand forecasting algorithms trained on past data struggled to predict the significant shift in consumer behavior. Businesses that employed adaptive AI models altered their supply networks in real time, cutting losses.

2. Cybersecurity Requires AI That Can Detect New Threats.

Cybercriminals continually create new attack strategies. If AI-powered fraud detection systems rely on old attack patterns, they fail to stop modern threats.

Example: Mastercard uses an adaptive AI fraud detection system that examines patterns of suspicious activity and learns new fraudulent behaviors as they occur.

3. Autonomous Systems Need to Make Decisions in Unpredictable Situations.

A self-driving automobile cannot be pre-programmed for every possible road circumstance. It must adapt in real time.

Example: Waymo's autonomous vehicles use a reinforcement learning approach, where the AI learns from real-world driving data. When it faces new impediments, it adapts its behavior instead of relying on pre-existing rules.

Without adaptability, AI systems become liabilities instead of assets.

Key Technologies That Enable AI Adaptability.

Developing adaptive AI involves specialized technical approaches and technology. Some of the most effective strategies include:

1. Transfer Learning.

Instead of building an AI model from scratch, transfer learning allows it to apply expertise from one task to another.

Example: AI algorithms trained to detect cats and dogs may be swiftly fine-tuned to distinguish wild animals using minimum additional data.

How it aids adaptability: AI models generalize knowledge, making them usable in new settings without thorough retraining.

2. Reinforcement Learning

This technique allows AI to learn from its own experiences by earning rewards or punishments based on its judgments.

Example: OpenAI's robotic hand learned to manipulate items in real time by continuously refining its motor control techniques.

How it helps adaptability: AI can improve itself without human assistance, making it appropriate for changing contexts.

3. Automated Machine Learning (AutoML).

Instead of engineers manually refining AI models, AutoML automates the process, optimizing performance depending on new data.

Example: Google's AutoML can improve deep learning architectures without requiring AI professionals to make manual tweaks.

How it helps adaptability: AI systems self-optimize, ensuring they remain successful as data changes.

4. Federated Learning.

Instead of building AI models on centralized data, federated learning allows numerous devices to learn together while keeping data private.

Example: Google's Gourd keyboard AI learns from users' typing behavior across millions of smartphones, boosting accuracy without storing personal data on a central server.

How it aids adaptability: AI models learn from distributed sources, making them more responsive to real-world variances.

These technologies constitute the cornerstone of self-improving AI systems.

How Engineers Can Build More Adaptable AI.

If AI is to be truly adaptive, developers must follow best practices that assure long-term scalability, adaptability, and resilience.

1. Design AI Models with Modular Architectures.

Example: Cloud-based AI services like AWS SageMaker allow models to be updated without rewriting entire systems.

2. Implement Real-Time Feedback Loops.

Example: Facebook's ad-targeting AI regularly adapts based on user interaction patterns.

3. Use Hybrid AI Models.

Example: Combining rule-based reasoning with deep learning allows AI to evolve while being interpretable.

Building adaptive AI demands engineering discipline and the necessary infrastructure.

AI flexibility is not a luxury—it is a must for any system that must operate in fast-changing situations. Businesses that rely on static AI models will struggle, while those who invest in agility will stay ahead.

1.2 Principles of Scalable and Modular AI Code.

Artificial intelligence is being integrated into sectors at an unprecedented scale. From autonomous systems and financial predictions to healthcare diagnostics and tailored suggestions, AI is guiding decisions across sectors. However, one of the largest issues developers have is ensuring that AI code remains scalable and modular as systems expand in complexity.

A well-structured AI system should be able to handle increasing workloads, integrate new features without compromising existing functionality, and adapt to changing business needs. Without scalability and modularity, AI models become inefficient, hard to maintain, and expensive to update.

This section focuses on the key ideas that make AI programming scalable and modular, ensuring that it remains efficient, versatile, and ready for long-term use.

Why Scalability Matters in AI Development.

Scalability assures that an AI system can manage increased data volumes, greater user demands, and more complicated computations without a loss in performance. Poorly built AI models may operate well during testing but struggle under real-world settings.

Current Challenges That Demand Scalability.

1. AI-Powered Search and Recommendation Systems.

Platforms like Amazon, Netflix, and YouTube process vast quantities of user data every second. If their AI models were not scalable, recommendations would become slower, outdated, and meaningless.

2. Real-Time Fraud Detection in Banking.

Financial organizations rely on AI to detect fraudulent transactions instantaneously. A model that works well on a few thousand transactions per second may fail when processing millions of transactions over numerous locations.

3. AI in Healthcare Diagnostics.

Medical AI systems trained on restricted datasets may fail to generalize when applied to different populations. Scalable

AI ensures that as more patient data is collected, the system can refine its accuracy without requiring complete retraining.

Scalability is not only about processing greater datasets—it is about ensuring that AI systems continue to work efficiently under real-world settings.

Principles of Scalable AI Code.

To design scalable AI systems, developers must follow fundamental coding and architectural principles that allow AI models to evolve without performance bottlenecks.

1. Distributed Computing and Parallel Processing.

Scalable AI systems employ distributed computing frameworks like Apache Spark, TensorFlow, and PyTorch to process massive datasets efficiently. Instead of conducting computations on a single server, these frameworks divide workloads over numerous workstations or GPUs.

Example: OpenAI's ChatGPT processes millions of questions daily. This is possible because it runs on a distributed architecture that scales dynamically to satisfy global demand.

Best Practice: Use horizontal scaling— adding many machines to a network rather than relying on a single high-powered server—to assure stability and efficiency.

2. Stateless and Asynchronous Processing.

Traditional AI applications generally suffer with scaling because they rely on tasteful processing, where each operation depends on prior computations. Scalable AI utilizes a stateless design, allowing independent tasks to operate in parallel.

Example: Google's AI-powered search indexing processes web pages independently, making it possible to handle billions of new pages every day without slowing down.

Best Practice: Use asynchronous processing to handle tasks in parallel rather than waiting for one process to complete before initiating the next.

3. API-First Architecture for AI Services.

Instead of constructing monolithic AI apps, developers should design modular AI services that communicate over APIs. This makes it easier to integrate AI models into many platforms and applications.

Example: Facebook's AI models for facial recognition, spam detection, and ad targeting function as independent micro services, making it easier to change one model without impacting the others.

Best Practice: Build AI as standalone API services, allowing various teams to work on separate models without affecting the entire system.

By adopting these principles, AI systems can scale efficiently without requiring new redesigns every time demand increases.

Why Modularity is Essential for AI Development.

Modular AI programming breaks down large models into smaller, reusable components, making it easier to manage, debug, and update.

A modular AI system allows developers to:

Swap out components without altering the entire model.

Reuse existing code for new projects.

Speed up development by working on distinct components simultaneously.

Examples of Modular AI in Action.

1. Self-Driving Cars.

AI for autonomous vehicles consists of numerous distinct modules: object identification, path planning, sensor fusion, and decision-making. If one module improves (e.g., better pedestrian recognition), it can be updated without retraining the entire system.

2. AI-Powered Virtual Assistants.

Amazon Alexa, Google Assistant, and Apple Siri use modular AI to handle speech recognition, language processing, and response generation separately. This allows new languages, accents, and voice commands to be added without affecting existing functions.

3. AI in Enterprise Applications.

Large-scale enterprises utilize AI models for customer care chatbots, fraud detection, and tailored marketing—all of which run as autonomous AI modules communicating through APIs.

Modularity guarantees that AI systems stay flexible and adaptable as business requirements grow.

Principles of Modular AI Code

Developing modular AI systems demands organized coding standards and unambiguous separation of concerns.

1. Encapsulation of AI Components.

Each AI function should be packaged as a distinct module that can be updated or modified without affecting the complete system.

Example: In AI-powered email spam detection, different modules handle feature extraction, categorization, and user feedback learning. If a better classification method emerges, it can be included without affecting the feature extraction process.

2. Model Versioning and Rollback Strategies.

AI models are regularly updated, but upgrades must be managed carefully to avoid damaging existing functionality.

Example: Microsoft Azure AI enables version management for AI models, allowing businesses to roll back to a previous version if an update produces errors.

Best Practice: Implement model versioning so that new upgrades do not interrupt production systems.

3. Standardized Interfaces and Data Pipelines.

A modular AI system should use standardized interfaces and data pipelines to allow easy communication between different AI modules.

Example: Google's TensorFlow Extended (TFX) provides a common framework for data ingestion, model training, and deployment, making it easier to combine multiple AI components.

Best Practice: Use well-defined APIs and data standards to guarantee AI modules can interact seamlessly.

These concepts enable AI systems to evolve over time without substantial interruptions.

How Scalability and Modularity Work Together.

Scalability and modularity are not different concepts—they encourage each other. A scalable AI system must also be modular to avoid inefficiencies.

Example: Large-scale AI applications like Google Translate use a modular neural network architecture that allows language models to be changed independently while maintaining scalability.

Example: Tesla's AI-powered self-driving software uses a modular perception system that processes sensor data independently. This allows Tesla to introduce new features without retraining the entire AI layer.

By combining scalability and modularity, AI systems can withstand large-scale deployments while staying flexible and easy to maintain.

AI systems that fail to scale become inefficient, and those that lack modularity become costly and difficult to update. Whether designing AI for real-time analytics, autonomous systems, or enterprise applications, engineers must focus on constructing scalable and modular code.

By applying distributed computing, API-first architectures, encapsulated AI components, and model versioning, developers can create AI systems that remain efficient, adaptable, and future-proof.

1.3 Designing Reusable AI Components.

As AI systems grow in complexity, software engineers and data scientists face the challenge of maintaining efficiency while keeping costs and development time under control. One of the most effective ways to achieve this is by designing reusable AI components—modules, functions, or services that can be applied across different projects without requiring significant modifications.

Reusable AI components reduce redundancy, improve scalability, and ensure consistency across different applications. Instead of constructing every AI model or feature from scratch, businesses can reuse well-tested components to speed up development, boost dependability, and decrease computational cost.

Why Reusable AI Components Matter.

Many AI-powered services operate at a vast scale, managing billions of interactions every day. Without reusability, engineers would have to rebuild essential functionalities repeatedly, leading to wasted resources.

For example:

Google's AI models for speech recognition, text translation, and search ranking have common neural network components. Instead of developing a fresh AI model for every use case, Google engineers reuse elements of current models to enhance efficiency and accuracy.

Tesla's self-driving AI includes modular components for lane detection, pedestrian recognition, and object tracking. Each component is designed to be independent and reusable, allowing developers to modify one area without affecting the overall system.

Netflix's recommendation engine relies on reusable data pipelines and machine learning models across multiple content categories. Whether recommending movies, TV series, or documentaries, the core AI components remain the same, enhancing the development pace.

These examples show how reusability helps AI systems remain efficient, versatile, and easy to upgrade without considerable rework.

Core Principles of Reusable AI Components.

Building reusable AI components involves careful design and deliberate execution. Components should be modular, adaptive, and autonomous to ensure they can be merged into multiple AI projects without major alterations.

1. Modular Architecture.

A reusable AI component should function independently, meaning it does not depend on the internal logic of other elements of the system.

Example: In an AI Chabot, natural language processing (NLP) and sentiment analysis can be constructed as independent modules. If a firm wants to add a new language model, it can replace the NLP component without affecting sentiment analysis.

Best Practice: Use micro services architecture, where AI functionalities operate as independent services that interact through APIs. This enables seamless updating and integration into other apps.

2. Generalized Models with Customization.

Reusable AI components should be created with flexibility in mind. Instead of hardcoding functionality for a given use case, developers should construct models that can be fine-tuned for other applications.

Example: OpenAI's GPT models are trained on a broad dataset and then fine-tuned for specific tasks like customer support, content development, or coding assistance. This strategy allows firms to reuse the same AI model for numerous functions without retraining from scratch.

Best Practice: Train AI models with transfer learning, allowing them to adapt to new tasks with minimal extra training.

3. Standardized Data Pipelines.

AI components rely on data, and if the data formats or input architectures vary between projects, reuse becomes difficult. Standardized data pipelines ensure that AI models can process information consistently, regardless of where they are deployed.

Example: Financial institutions deploy AI models for fraud detection across different payment systems. By standardizing transaction data formats, businesses may reuse the same fraud detection algorithm across credit cards, bank transfers, and online payments.

Best Practice: Implement feature stores, centralized repositories that store and manage AI-ready data to maintain consistency across models.

4. Interoperability and API Design.

To make AI components reusable across many platforms, they should be developed with clear interfaces and API compatibility.

Example: AI-powered recommendation engines, like Spotify's music suggestions, are created as standalone services that connect with multiple apps via APIs. This allows Spotify to integrate AI-powered suggestions across online apps, mobile apps, and even smart speakers without altering the main algorithm.

Best Practice: Use RESTful APIs or GraphQL to provide seamless communication between AI components and multiple platforms.

Building Blocks of Reusable AI Components.

To create efficient reusable AI components, developers must focus on modularity at various levels—from individual functions to entire machine learning models.

1. Reusable Preprocessing Functions.

Every AI model requires data preprocessing, but instead of developing new code for each project, typical activities like data cleaning, normalization, and feature engineering may be packaged into reusable functions.

Example: A face recognition AI system can contain a repeatable preprocessing function that automatically adjusts image brightness, removes noise, and aligns facial features before providing the data to the model.

Best Practice: Store reusable preprocessing functions in a centralized code repository to maintain consistency across projects.

2. Reusable Machine Learning Models.

Machine learning models developed on huge datasets can be repurposed for numerous purposes through fine-tuning.

Example: A sentiment analysis model trained for social media can be fine-tuned to analyze customer reviews without creating a new dataset from scratch.

Best Practice: Implement model versioning so that modifications to a reusable AI model do not interrupt existing applications.

3. Reusable Deployment Pipelines.

AI components should be packaged in a way that allows them to be deployed across diverse environments without modification.

Example: AI-driven fraud detection models in banking need to be implemented across cloud servers, mobile applications, and on-premise databases. A reusable deployment pipeline means that the same model can be easily rolled out across various platforms.

Best Practice: Use containerization (Docker, Kubernetes) to make AI models portable across diverse infrastructures.

Real-World Examples of Reusable AI Components.

1. Google's AI for Image Recognition.

Google's image recognition AI, used in Google Photos, Google Lens, and autonomous vehicles, relies on a single deep learning model. This model can recognize objects, text, and scenarios, but its modular nature allows it to be customized for diverse use cases.

Impact: Developers across several teams can utilize the same basic AI model for diverse products without retraining from scratch.

2. Microsoft Azure AI Services.

Microsoft delivers pre-trained AI models for speech recognition, text analytics, and facial recognition through its Azure AI services. Businesses can integrate these AI capabilities into their own apps without needing to construct new models.

Impact: Companies can speed AI adoption by adopting Microsoft's reusable AI components instead of training custom models from the ground up.

3. Tesla's Autopilot Software.

Tesla's self-driving AI uses a modular approach where distinct AI components handle lane detection, traffic sign recognition, and collision avoidance separately. These components can be changed independently, making it easier to bring out new features without retraining the entire system.

Impact: Tesla can deploy regular AI updates to improve driving performance without disturbing the overall system.

Challenges in Designing Reusable AI Components.

While reusability brings numerous benefits, it also comes with challenges:

1. Balancing Generalization and Specialization.

A reusable AI component should be flexible enough to handle multiple use cases but not so generic that it loses efficacy.

Solution: Use adjustable parameters that allow AI components to be adjusted for individual applications without requiring extensive retraining.

2. Maintaining Compatibility across Platforms.

Different AI systems may employ different programming languages, frameworks, and hardware.

Solution: Ensure AI components support standardized file formats and communication protocols to work across multiple contexts.

3. Security and Data Privacy Risks.

Reusable AI components may process sensitive information, presenting significant security problems.

Solution: Implement strong encryption, access controls, and compliance checks to protect AI models and user data.

Reusable AI components save time, decrease costs, and improve consistency across AI-driven systems. Whether used in recommendation engines, self-driving cars, fraud detection, or virtual assistants, modular AI components allow businesses to innovate faster while maintaining high performance and dependability.

By focusing on modular architecture, standardized APIs, model versioning, and flexible data pipelines, AI developers can build systems that scale effectively and remain adaptable for years to come.

Chapter 2: Advanced Machine Learning Architectures.

2.1 Implementing Transformer-Based Models.

Artificial intelligence has made enormous progress over the years, and at the heart of many recent AI advances are transformer-based models. These models have redefined how robots process language, make visuals, and even assist in medication development. Unlike standard machine learning models that struggle with long-term dependencies, transformers efficiently manage enormous volumes of sequential data. Their capacity to understand complicated patterns has made them the backbone of today's most powerful AI systems, from OpenAI's GPT to Google's BERT and DeepMind's AlphaFold.

Implementing transformer-based models needs a detailed understanding of their architecture, optimization methodologies, and real-world applications. These models are computationally expensive, but when applied successfully, they can fuel advanced AI systems across industries.

The Core Structure of Transformer Models.

Transformers are built on a self-attention mechanism, which allows them to process full sequences of data simultaneously rather than step by step. This makes them significantly more efficient than prior models like recurrent neural networks (RNNs) or long short-term memory (LSTM) networks.

The key components of a transformer model include

1. Multi-Head Self-Attention: Helps the model identify relationships between words or data points, even when they are far away.

2. Positional Encoding: Since transformers do not process data sequentially like RNNs, positional encoding helps them comprehend the order of elements.

3. Feed forward Layers: Fully connected neural networks that refine the information extracted from self-attention layers.

4. Layer Normalization: Ensures stable learning and prevents performance degradation.

5. Residual Connections: Helps maintain gradient flow, making deep transformers easier to train.

These components enable transformers to retain long-range dependencies, making them highly effective for tasks such as natural language processing, code generation, and image recognition.

Implementing a Transformer Model from Scratch.

To build a transformer-based model, developers typically rely on deep learning frameworks like TensorFlow or PyTorch. Let's break down the steps required to implement a basic transformer.

Step 1: Preparing the Data.

Transformers require well-structured data, whether it's text, images, or numerical sequences.

For example, in language modeling, a dataset of text needs to be tokenized into numerical representations. This process involves:

Tokenization: Splitting text into words, subwords, or characters.

Embedding: Converting tokens into dense vectors using pre-trained embedding or learned representations.

Libraries like Hugging Face's Transformers provide sophisticated tokenizes that facilitate this procedure.

Step 2: Defining the Self-Attention Mechanism.

Self-attention is the core of a transformer. Instead of processing words in order, it enables the model to weigh the importance of different parts of a sequence.

The attention mechanism works by computing:

Query (Q), Key (K), and Value (V) matrices from input embedding's.

Attention scores that determine the influence of one word on others.

Weighted summation to construct meaningful representations.

This helps the model to interpret context more effectively than earlier systems.

Step 3: Stacking Transformer Layers.

A transformer consists of numerous encoder and decoder layers.

Each encoder layer includes:

Multi-head self-attention to process relationships within the input.

Feedforward layers to refine learned characteristics.

Layer normalization and dropout to stabilize training.

The decoder follows a similar layout but includes additional cross-attention layers to interact with encoded information.

Step 4: Training the Model.

Training transformers requires:

Large-scale datasets (e.g., Wikipedia for language models).

Substantial processing power, generally employing GPUs or TPUs.

Optimization strategies include AdamW and learning rate scheduling.

Training a model from scratch is resource-intensive, which is why many AI practitioners employ pre-trained transformers and fine-tune them for specific applications.

Optimizing Transformer-Based Models for Efficiency.

Transformers are powerful but expensive in terms of computation. Optimizing them ensures they remain useful for real-world applications.

1. Reducing Computational Costs.

One of the main issues with transformers is their high memory and processing requirements. Strategies to cut costs include:

Efficient attention methods like Linformer and Performer, which mimic self-attention while utilizing fewer resources.

Quantization strategies that reduce model precision (e.g., using 8-bit instead of 32-bit floating points) to speed up inference.

Distillation, where a large transformer trains a smaller model, keeping accuracy while reducing processing needs.

2. Scaling Up Using Parallelization.

Many firms employ transformer-based AI across numerous GPUs or cloud-based infrastructure. Model parallelism allows various elements of a transformer to be handled on distinct machines, enhancing training speed.

For example, Meta's LLaMA models employ distributed training across hundreds of GPUs, allowing them to handle enormous datasets while preserving efficiency.

3. Handling Real-World Constraints.

AI-powered applications, such as voice assistants or mobile AI models, require transformers that run effectively on edge devices. Techniques like pruning (removing extraneous model weights) and sparse attention assist in making transformer models lightweight for mobile and embedded systems.

Real-World Applications of Transformer Models.

1. Natural Language Processing (NLP) and Chatbots.

Large-scale transformer models are commonly employed in NLP applications such as:

Chatbots and virtual assistants (e.g., ChatGPT, Google Bard) that provide human-like responses.

Language translation (e.g., Google Translate) is enabled by models like BERT and T5.

Text summary for study and journalism, improving how we process enormous volumes of information.

2. AI-Powered Code Generation.

Transformers have changed software development with technologies like

GitHub Copilot, which offers code completions and automates repetitive programming activities.

AlphaCode, developed by DeepMind, solves competitive programming issues using transformer-based models.

3. Medical and Scientific Research.

Transformers are being utilized in healthcare for:

Protein structure prediction, as demonstrated in AlphaFold, has transformed biochemistry by predicting molecular structures.

Medical diagnostics and drug discovery, where AI analyzes patient data to recommend therapies.

4. Autonomous Systems and Robotics.

Self-driving cars and robotics benefit from transformers through:

Vision Transformers (ViTs) for object detection and scene interpretation.

Multimodal transformers mix text, pictures, and sensor data to assist AI decision-making.

Challenges in Implementing Transformer-Based Models.

While transformers have transformed AI, they come with their own set of challenges:

1. High Training Costs.

Training big transformers involves massive datasets and powerful technology.

Solution: Use pre-trained models and fine-tune them on specific tasks.

2. Ethical and Bias Concerns.

AI models might inherit biases from the data they are trained on.

Solution: Implement bias detection and fairness audits during training.

3. Interpretability Issues.

Unlike simpler models, transformers serve as "black boxes," making it impossible to grasp their decision-making process.

Solution: Develop explainable AI (XAI) techniques to comprehend model results.

4. Energy Consumption.

Large AI models require enormous electricity, posing ecological problems.

Solution: Optimize transformers with efficient designs and green AI approaches.

Transformer-based models have altered artificial intelligence, enabling breakthroughs in language processing, software development, healthcare, and robotics. Their capacity to analyze large-scale data efficiently and adapt to varied applications has made them indispensable.

As technology progresses, the future of transformers will likely emphasize efficiency, ethical AI, and real-world flexibility. Engineers and academics are continuously refining these models to ensure they remain at the forefront of intelligent computing.

2.2 Optimizing Neural Network Structures for Adaptability.

Artificial intelligence continues to evolve at an astonishing pace, driven mostly by neural networks. However, as the complexity of AI systems develops, so does the requirement for adaptation. A neural network that cannot respond to new data, unforeseen circumstances, or real-world obstacles would fast become obsolete. The key to constructing powerful AI systems is in designing neural network architectures for adaptability.

Adaptable neural networks are capable of responding to changing surroundings, learning from limited input, and improving over time without constant human involvement. This skill is vital for businesses ranging from driverless vehicles to tailored healthcare and fraud detection.

Building adaptive neural networks involves the appropriate architectural decisions, effective training approaches, and mechanisms that allow AI models to function in ever-changing situations.

Understanding Adaptability in Neural Networks.

Adaptability in neural networks refers to their ability to:

Generalize to unseen data without overfitting.

Adjust model parameters dynamically when new information becomes available.

Work efficiently across diverse hardware and software environments.

Handle real-world noise, uncertainty, and unexpected patterns.

This adaptability is crucial in applications like self-driving cars, which must swiftly understand new road conditions, or financial fraud detection, where AI must recognize growing patterns of questionable activity.

There are various architectural options and optimization methodologies that can increase a neural network's ability to adapt.

1. Modular Neural Network Design.

Traditional neural networks are generally trained as monolithic models, meaning every element of the network contributes to every job. However, modularity offers greater flexibility. A modular neural network consists of different components, each responsible for a specific purpose.

Benefits of Modular Neural Networks:

Faster adaptation: Instead of retraining the entire model, individual modules can be fine-tuned independently.

Efficient problem-solving: Different modules can specialize in different tasks, enhancing performance.

Scalability: New modules can be added without impacting existing functionality.

For example, Tesla's Full Self-Driving (FSD) technology adopts a modular approach. One module performs lane detection, another predicts pedestrian movement, while another interprets traffic signals. This allows Tesla to update certain elements of the system without retraining the entire neural network.

Implementation Strategy:

Design independent sub-networks for distinct tasks.

Use a controller network to pick which modules to activate based on the input.

Train components separately and then merge them into a unified framework.

2. Dynamic Neural Networks (DNNs).

Dynamic neural networks modify their structure based on input data. Unlike traditional static models, which maintain a set architecture, DNNs can expand, contract, or rearrange themselves in response to new problems.

How Dynamic Networks Improve Adaptability:

Elastic Capacity: Networks can grow while handling complicated tasks and shrink when executing simpler ones, optimizing resource utilization.

Task-Specific Learning: Different architectures might be implemented based on the complexity of the incoming data.

Real-Time Adjustments: Networks can prioritize critical information while discarding unnecessary details.

A real-world example is Google's DeepMind AlphaGo, which dynamically altered its strategy based on an opponent's movements rather than relying on a predefined rule set. This ability to adapt strategy in real time made it capable of beating world-class human players.

Implementation Strategy:

Use Neural Architecture Search (NAS) to design flexible architectures.

Implement attention-based mechanisms that focus on the most relevant information dynamically.

Allow layer-wise adaptation, where certain layers are frozen while others remain trainable.

3. Self-Supervised Learning for Continuous Adaptation.

Traditional supervised learning relies on huge, labeled datasets, while real-world AI systems must adapt without ongoing human supervision. Self-supervised learning (SSL) allows neural networks to create their own learning signals from raw, unlabeled data.

Advantages of Self-Supervised Learning:

Reduces dependency on labeled data, making training faster and more cost-effective.

Improves generalization, as models learn from different, unstructured inputs.

Enhances transfer learning, enabling AI to apply knowledge from one domain to another.

For instance, Meta's DINO (self-supervised vision transformer) trains image recognition models without labeled data, enabling AI to identify images with minimal human participation. Similarly, huge language models like GPT-4 enhance their knowledge without direct supervision, making them more versatile across varied applications.

Implementation Strategy:

Use contrastive learning, where a model learns by differentiating between similar and dissimilar examples.

Train models using prediction tasks, such as filling in missing information from input data.

Leverage unsupervised pretraining, followed by task-specific fine-tuning.

4. Optimizing Hyperparameters for Adaptability.

Hyperparameter tuning is one of the most crucial components of optimizing neural networks. Instead of depending on static hyperparameters, AI systems should alter parameters dynamically based on task complexity and data qualities.

Techniques for Adaptive Hyperparameter Tuning:

1. **Bayesian Optimization**—Selects hyperparameters intelligently instead of searching blindly.

2. **Gradient-Based Tuning**—adjusts learning rates and other parameters dynamically during training.

3. **Meta-Learning (Learning to Learn)**— Teaches neural networks how to optimize their own hyperparameters.

For example, OpenAI's reinforcement learning agent's use meta-learning to optimize learning rates based on previous performance, allowing them to train efficiently in changing environments.

Implementation Strategy:

Use automated hyperparameter search frameworks like Optuna or Hyperopt.

Allow networks to dynamically alter dropout rates, activation functions, and layer depths based on model performance.

Implement adaptive learning rate schedules, such as cosine annealing or cyclical learning rates.

5. Incorporating Attention Mechanisms for Context Awareness.

Attention mechanisms greatly improve the adaptability of neural networks by helping models focus on the most relevant input while disregarding unnecessary aspects.

Types of Attention That Improve Adaptability:

Self-Attention: Used in transformers to identify relationships between data points.

Spatial Attention: Helps vision models focus on specific portions of an image.

Temporal Attention: Allows sequential models to prioritize relevant time-based events.

Modern AI models like ChatGPT and Bard rely on transformer-based attention mechanisms to provide human-like answers by dynamically ranking significant words in a phrase. Similarly, in medical imaging, attention layers reveal abnormalities in X-rays, enhancing diagnosis accuracy.

Implementation Strategy:

Integrate multi-head attention layers to boost adaptability.

Use adaptive attention scores that alter depending on input complexity.

Apply context-aware gating methods to refine model predictions dynamically.

6. Efficient Memory Management for Long-Term Adaptability.

AI systems generally struggle with long-term memory retention, making it difficult for them to adjust over time. Memory-efficient neural networks promote adaptability by storing old knowledge while integrating new information.

Techniques for Memory Optimization:

Long Short-Term Memory (LSTM) & Gated Recurrent Units (GRUs)—Allow networks to retain relevant information over extended durations.

Memory-Augmented Networks (MANNs)—Store external knowledge that AI models can retrieve when needed.

Experience Replay in Reinforcement Learning—Helps AI recall and apply past learning to new situations.

Self-driving cars, for instance, deploy memory-based AI models to recall previous driving circumstances and apply them to real-time navigation.

Implementation Strategy:

Use replay buffers to store and recover past experiences.

Implement hierarchical memory architectures for greater long-term retention.

Combine episodic memory networks with typical deep learning models.

Optimizing neural network architectures for flexibility is vital for constructing scalable, intelligent, and self-optimizing AI systems. The most effective AI models are those that

Adjust dynamically to new challenges.

Efficiently manage computational resources.

Learn with minimal supervision.

Retain long-term knowledge.

By adding modular designs, self-supervised learning, attention mechanisms, dynamic structures, and adaptive hyperparameter tuning, AI developers may ensure that neural networks stay highly functional in real-world applications.

2.3 Hybrid AI Systems: Combining Rule-Based and Learning-Based Approaches.

Artificial intelligence has altered industries, from healthcare to banking, by making data-driven choices at unprecedented speeds. However, no single AI technique is flawless. Traditional rule-based systems offer predictability and structure, while learning-based models provide flexibility and adaptability. To construct AI that is both dependable and scalable, modern systems are increasingly merging these two methodologies into hybrid AI models.

A hybrid AI system integrates rule-based reasoning with machine learning to provide higher performance, adaptability, and efficiency. This approach is particularly beneficial in contexts where pure machine learning models may lack transparency or where established rules alone cannot handle complex scenarios.

Industries like autonomous driving, fraud detection, and healthcare diagnostics rely on hybrid AI systems to boost decision-making, minimize errors, and improve flexibility. By mixing rigid rules with machine learning's power to spot patterns, hybrid AI builds self-optimizing and context-aware systems.

Understanding Hybrid AI Systems.

To completely grasp the value of hybrid AI, it is vital to understand its two fundamental components:

1. Rule-Based Systems.

Operate on predefined "if-then" logic.

Provide transparency and predictable decision-making.

Work well in structured areas with established conditions.

Example: A bank's fraud detection system that bans transactions over a specific amount.

2. Learning-Based Systems (Machine Learning & Deep Learning).

Identify patterns in data to make predictions.

Adapt to fresh information over time.

Handle complicated, dynamic contexts where rigid rules may fail.

Example: A credit card fraud detection AI that learns from prior fraudulent transactions to detect new ones.

Hybrid AI integrates these two paradigms, allowing systems to be both organized and adaptive.

Why Hybrid AI Systems Are Necessary.

Machine learning models can forecast and adapt, yet they often suffer from:

Lack of transparency—it can be difficult to explain why a model made a given decision.

High computational expenses—Training deep learning models takes massive amounts of data and computer power.

Data dependency—ML models suffer in low-data contexts or where real-time learning is needed.

On the other side, rule-based systems can maintain consistency, but them:

Do not learn—once deployed, they cannot adapt to fresh data.

Struggle with complexity—writing rules for every scenario is impractical.

By incorporating both methodologies, hybrid AI systems can give organized decision-making with the potential to learn and improve.

Real-World Applications of Hybrid AI Systems.

1. Fraud Detection in Banking and Finance.

Financial fraud detection is a classic illustration of how hybrid AI helps decision-making.

Rule-Based Approach: Banks have static rules (e.g., transactions over $10,000 prompt a manual check).

Machine Learning Approach: AI examines transaction history to find anomalous patterns.

A hybrid AI fraud detection system:

Uses rule-based filters to block obvious fraudulent actions.

Employs ML models to detect subtle fraud tendencies, such as tiny unlawful withdrawals that increase over time.

For example, Visa and Mastercard deploy hybrid AI models to evaluate billions of transactions in real time, lowering false positives and enhancing fraud detection accuracy.

2. Healthcare Diagnostics and Treatment Recommendations.

Healthcare AI must balance rigorous restrictions with real-time adaptability.

Rule-Based Approach: Follows medical guidelines to diagnose illnesses.

Machine Learning Approach: Analyzes patient history and medical imaging to find problems.

A mixed AI system in healthcare might:

Use rule-based decision trees to guarantee medical protocols are followed.

Apply ML models to discover uncommon diseases that do not suit standard criteria.

For example, IBM's Watson for Oncology combines medical rules with AI-driven insights to offer individualized cancer treatments.

3. Autonomous Vehicles and Smart Transportation.

Self-driving cars rely on AI to navigate difficult road conditions safely.

Rule-Based Approach: Traffic laws (e.g., stopping at red lights, yielding to pedestrians).

Machine Learning Approach: AI learns from millions of driving instances to predict behavior.

A hybrid AI driving system:

Uses predefined traffic rules for consistent behavior.

Leverages ML models to adjust to unforeseen occurrences (e.g., pedestrians jaywalking).

Tesla's Autopilot and Full Self-Driving (FSD) system is a hybrid AI example. It follows stringent driving regulations but regularly upgrades itself based on real-world data.

Key Components of a Hybrid AI System

Building a successful hybrid AI system requires:

1. A Clear Decision Framework.

Define when the system should employ rules vs. machine learning.

Example: A Chabot may employ rule-based responses for FAQs but ML for natural language processing.

2. A Feedback Loop for Continuous Learning.

The system should improve rules over time based on fresh data and model outputs.

Example: If a fraud detection system flags too many false positives, it should alter its criteria dynamically.

3. Interoperability between Rule Engines and ML Models.

AI systems must be able to effortlessly move between rule-based and ML-driven decision-making.

Example: A hybrid cybersecurity system that enforces static firewall rules but also detects novel threats using ML.

4. Transparency and Explainability Mechanisms.

Hybrid AI should provide explainable decisions to build confidence.

Example: AI-generated medical diagnoses should be complemented with rule-based reasons for doctors.

Challenges in Implementing Hybrid AI Systems.

Despite its advantages, hybrid AI confronts issues that must be addressed:

1. Complexity in System Design.

Integrating rule-based logic with ML models requires careful architecture planning.

Solution: Use modular design to keep AI components adaptable and scalable.

2. Balancing Adaptability with Stability.

Too many rules can impede learning, while too much ML can induce unpredictability.

Solution: Define clear decision limits where rules take precedence over ML.

3. Handling Edge Cases and Bias.

Rule-based systems may not cover all circumstances, whereas ML models can inherit biases from training data.

Solution: Continuously audit and update both rule sets and ML parameters.

Best Practices for Developing Hybrid AI Systems.

To design effective hybrid AI models, developers should:

1. Use a Layered Approach.

Design separate layers for rules and ML to ensure smooth interaction.

2. Optimize for Performance and Scalability.

Ensure hybrid AI runs efficiently on edge devices, cloud servers, and local systems.

3. Implement Continuous Monitoring and Feedback.

Deploy real-time analytics to monitor how well rules and ML models function together.

4. Keep Humans in the Loop.

Use AI-assisted decision-making instead of full automation for high-risk applications.

Hybrid AI systems are vital for constructing adaptive, intelligent, and self-optimizing AI solutions. By merging rule-based logic with learning-based techniques, AI may preserve structure while continuously improving over time.

Industries like banking, healthcare, cybersecurity, and autonomous vehicles are already benefiting from hybrid AI's ability to mix precision with flexibility. Moving forward, AI engineers must optimize hybrid systems to maximize performance, transparency, and efficiency.

Chapter 3: Adaptive AI Algorithms and Optimization.

3.1 Dynamic Hyperparameter Tuning and AutoML.

Artificial intelligence has altered industries by enabling machines to learn, forecast, and optimize decision-making processes. However, the efficiency of AI models depends largely on the hyperparameters that control their training and performance. Choosing the correct hyperparameters—such as learning rates, batch sizes, and model architectures—can mean the difference between a well-performing AI system and one that fails to generalize to real-world data.

Traditionally, manual hyperparameter tuning required data scientists to experiment through trial and error, frequently requiring significant time and computer resources. Today, dynamic hyperparameter tweaking and automated machine learning (AutoML) have made AI development more efficient, scalable, and adaptive. These strategies allow models to self-optimize, leading to higher performance with minimal human intervention.

Recent achievements in AI, such as Google's AutoML, Meta's self-tuning AI models, and Tesla's autonomous driving optimizations, underscore the relevance of adaptive tuning methods. As AI continues to change industries like healthcare, banking, and autonomous systems, dynamic hyperparameter tuning guarantees that models remain efficient, adaptive, and capable of managing new data patterns.

Understanding Hyperparameters and Their Role in AI.

To design a successful AI model, developers must configure both parameters and hyperparameters. While parameters (such as neural network weights) are learned during training, hyperparameters must be established before training begins. These include:

Learning Rate: Determines how much a model updates throughout training. A high learning rate may converge too rapidly, while a low rate may slow learning.

Batch Size: Controls how much data is processed at once. Smaller batches allow for more frequent updates but require more iterations.

Number of Layers & Neurons: Defines the architecture of deep learning models.

Regularization Factors: Helps minimize overfitting by limiting model complexity.

Hyperparameter tuning is critical since incorrect choices can lead to ineffective training, overfitting, or underfitting. Traditionally, selecting the proper values needed expertise and manual modifications, but today, AI itself can optimize these decisions dynamically.

Traditional vs. Dynamic Hyperparameter Tuning.

Before considering advanced optimization strategies, it is crucial to understand the constraints of classical hyperparameter tuning and how dynamic methods improve the process.

1. Manual Grid Search and Random Search.

Early methods for hyperparameter tweaking utilized grid search and random search:

Grid Search: Tests all possible combinations of hyperparameters within a set range. This method is exhaustive yet computationally expensive.

Random Search: Selects hyperparameter values at random, covering a broad range without investigating every candidate. This method is speedier but lacks efficiency.

While these strategies work for small-scale AI models, they become unfeasible for deep learning systems that require millions of alternative configurations.

2. Dynamic Hyperparameter Optimization.

Unlike static tuning methods, dynamic optimization updates hyperparameters in real-time as the model trains. This allows AI models to:

Adapt to dataset complexity without requiring predetermined ranges.

Optimize training speed and accuracy by altering parameters dynamically.

Reduce computational expenses by reducing needless trials.

Popular dynamic tuning methods include:

Bayesian Optimization.

Gradient-Based Hyperparameter Tuning.

Reinforcement Learning-Based Hyperparameter Adjustment.

Bayesian Optimization for AI Models.

One of the most effective strategies for dynamic tuning is Bayesian optimization, which represents hyperparameter tuning as a probabilistic process. Instead of aimlessly searching for the best values, Bayesian methods:

1. It uses prior knowledge from past experiments to forecast promising hyperparameter values.

2. Prioritize areas of high performance rather than evaluating every combination.

3. Continuously refine hyperparameters based on real-time model performance.

Example: AI-Powered Drug Discovery

Pharmaceutical businesses utilize Bayesian optimization to expedite drug discovery and protein folding studies. Instead of manually testing millions of molecule combinations, AI models continuously modify learning rates and model parameters to maximize chemical compound predictions.

Gradient-Based Hyperparameter Tuning.

Another technique for dynamic tuning is gradient-based optimization, which treats hyperparameters as learnable variables. Unlike static approaches, gradient-based tuning:

- Adjusts hyperparameters by back propagation.
- Adapts learning rates and model topologies based on real-time performance.
- Reduces training time by minimizing needless computations.
- This strategy is particularly beneficial in deep learning applications like natural language processing (NLP) and autonomous systems.

Example: Optimizing Large Language Models.

AI models like ChatGPT and Google Gemini require billions of hyperparameter tweaks. Manual tuning is difficult at this scale; thus, dynamic gradient-based tuning guarantees these models optimize themselves based on usage patterns and real-time input.

Reinforcement Learning-Based Hyperparameter Adjustment.

Reinforcement learning (RL) adds reward-based optimization to hyperparameter tuning. Instead of predefined tuning rules, the AI:

- Treats hyperparameter selection as a decision-making process.
- Receives feedback from model performance and adapts accordingly.
- Continuously optimizes hyperparameters depending on real-time model efficiency.

Example: AI in Financial Markets.

Financial institutions use RL-based hyperparameter tuning for algorithmic trading models. These AI-driven algorithms constantly modify hyperparameters to respond to market fluctuations, enhancing trade forecasts and lowering risk.

The Rise of AutoML: Automating the AI Development Process.

AutoML (Automated Machine Learning) is the next evolution of AI model creation. It automates:

Feature Selection—identifies the most relevant data inputs.

Model Selection—chooses the best method for a given task.

Hyperparameter Tuning—Optimizes parameters dynamically.

AutoML solutions, such as Google Cloud AutoML, Microsoft Azure ML, and Amazon SageMaker, make AI development more accessible by reducing human tuning difficulties.

Real-World Impact of AutoML.

1. Healthcare Diagnostics.

AI-powered medical imaging employs AutoML to fine-tune models for detecting diseases like cancer and diabetic retinopathy.

AutoML modifies hyperparameters based on patient data, enhancing diagnosis accuracy.

2. Self-Driving Cars.

AutoML enables autonomous vehicles to adapt learning parameters based on weather, traffic, and road conditions.

Tesla's FSD (Full Self-Driving) Beta regularly upgrades its AI models utilizing AutoML.

3. Cybersecurity and Threat Detection.

AutoML boosts cybersecurity by constantly modifying AI models to detect evolving threats in real-time.

AI-driven security organizations, such as Darktrace, employ AutoML to prevent cyberattacks with minimum human interaction.

Challenges and Considerations in Dynamic Tuning and AutoML.

Despite its advantages, dynamic hyperparameter tuning and AutoML bring challenges:

1. **Computational Costs**.

Dynamic tuning needs significant processing resources, making it expensive for large-scale AI models.

Solution: Use efficient optimization approaches, such as trimming low-impact hyperparameters.

2. **Overfitting Risks**.

AutoML may over-optimize for specialized datasets, lowering real-world generalization.

Solution: Implement cross-validation techniques to prevent overfitting.

3. Lack of Interpretability.

Dynamically tuned models can become black boxes, making it hard to comprehend why they made particular alterations.

Solution: Use explainable AI (XAI) approaches to promote transparency.

AI systems must be adaptive to handle continuously changing data and settings. Dynamic hyperparameter tweaking and AutoML represent a big leap in how AI models optimize themselves. From Bayesian optimization in drug development to AutoML in self-driving cars, these techniques are redefining machine learning efficiency and scalability. As AI continues to evolve, adaptive optimization methods will become critical for ensuring that models stay fast, accurate, and resource-efficient. Developers who integrate dynamic tuning and AutoML into their AI architectures will stay ahead in constructing scalable, intelligent, and self-optimizing systems.

3.2 Reinforcement Learning for Self-Improving AI.

Artificial intelligence systems are progressing beyond static models into self-improving creatures capable of adapting to new environments. At the heart of this revolution is reinforcement learning (RL)—a technology that enables AI to learn through trial and error, much like a human makes decisions based on experience. Unlike standard machine learning models that rely on predetermined datasets, RL-driven AI learns dynamically from its environment, modifying its actions based on feedback.

Reinforcement learning has produced revolutionary contributions to disciplines like robotics, finance, healthcare, and autonomous systems. Companies such as DeepMind, OpenAI, and Tesla are actively building RL-based models that continuously upgrade their decision-making capabilities. From AlphaGo's win against world champion Go players to self-learning robotic assistants in industrial automation, RL is determining the future of AI.

However, RL's power comes with limitations, including extensive training times, large computing needs, and unpredictable behaviors. To understand how reinforcement learning develops self-improving AI, it is crucial to explore how it works, its real-world applications, and the approaches that make it scalable and adaptive.

Understanding Reinforcement Learning:

How AI Learns Like Humans. Reinforcement learning is influenced by behavioral psychology, where learning occurs through a system of rewards and punishments. In RL, an AI agent interacts with an environment, executing activities that lead to either positive reinforcement (reward) or negative reinforcement (punishment). The goal is to maximize cumulative rewards over time by developing techniques.

An RL system consists of three fundamental components:

1. Agent: The AI system making decisions (e.g., a robot, trading algorithm, or Chabot).

2. Environment: The place where the agent acts and receives input (e.g., a game, financial market, or autonomous car simulation).

3. Reward Function: A scoring system that leads the agent's learning process (e.g., winning a game, making successful trades, or safely avoiding obstacles).

The AI improves by repeating trials and continuously changing its actions based on past experiences. Over time, it learns optimal techniques that maximize rewards.

Example: AI in Self-Driving Cars.

Autonomous vehicles employ RL to navigate uncertain traffic circumstances. A self-driving AI must:

- Decide whether to brake, accelerate, or change lanes depending on real-time data.
- Learn from previous driving experiences to better decision-making.
- Receive feedback from simulated wrecks or successful maneuvers, altering behavior accordingly.

Tesla's Full Self-Driving (FSD) system refines its algorithms using RL, allowing the AI to improve its driving capabilities without explicit programming for every circumstance.

Types of Reinforcement Learning Algorithms.

Different RL approaches assist AI systems in enhancing learning speed, efficiency, and adaptability. The most prevalent ways include:

1. Q-Learning (Model-Free RL).

Q-learning enables AI to learn optimal decision-making techniques without needing a predetermined model of the environment. The AI constructs a Q-table that links actions to expected rewards, refining decisions over time.

Used in robotic automation to optimize movement tactics.

Applied in game AI for decision-making in complex environments.

2. Deep Q-Networks (DQN).

DQN blends Q-learning with deep neural networks, allowing AI to manage big, complicated settings. Instead of manually storing every conceivable action, DQNs employ deep learning to approximate Q-values efficiently.

Powering AI-driven video game bots that continuously develop.

Enhancing AI-based medical diagnosis systems that refine forecasts.

3. Policy Gradient Methods.

Instead of predicting rewards for every conceivable action (like Q-learning), policy gradient approaches directly alter the AI's decision-making strategy using probability distributions.

Used in financial trading AI to alter investment strategy dynamically.

Applied in real-time strategy games to generate intelligent, developing opponents.

4. Actor-Critic Models.

A hybrid of Q-learning and policy gradients, Actor-Critic models use two networks:

The actor selects actions based on policy.

The Critic: Evaluates acts and provides comments.

This strategy enhances stability and efficiency in training, typically observed in robotic control systems and natural language processing (NLP) chatbots.

Real-World Applications of Reinforcement Learning.

Reinforcement learning is already altering sectors by enabling AI systems to make complicated judgments autonomously. Some of the more impactful applications include:

1. AI in Robotics: Teaching Machines to Adapt.

Industrial and service robots rely on RL to learn job automation, precision control, and real-world adaptability. Unlike programmed robots with fixed responses, RL-powered robots:

- Learn by trial and error instead of following exact directions.
- Improve efficiency through ongoing self-training.

Example: AI-Powered Factory Robots

Companies like Boston Dynamics and Tesla use RL to train robotic arms for manufacturing jobs. These robots refine their gripping, assembling, and welding abilities depending on real-time sensor feedback.

2. Reinforcement Learning in Finance: AI Traders and Market Predictions

Financial institutions utilize RL-powered AI models for algorithmic trading, portfolio management, and fraud detection. These AI traders:

- Continuously alter trading strategy based on market swings.
- Optimize investments by learning from prior financial data.
- Detect fraudulent transactions by recognizing unusual expenditure patterns.

Example: AI Trading Systems.

JPMorgan Chase and Goldman Sachs deploy RL-based AI for high-frequency trading. These systems make thousands of trades every second, learning from prior patterns to maximize earnings.

3. Healthcare AI: Adaptive Diagnosis and Treatment Plans.

Reinforcement learning is transforming personalized medicine by enabling AI systems to:

- Adjust cancer therapy procedures based on patient responses.
- Optimize drug discovery by simulating molecular interactions.
- Improve surgical robots, allowing them to adapt to complex procedures.

Example: AI in Cancer Treatment.

RL-driven AI helps physicians personalize chemotherapy regimens for patients. Instead of following static treatment plans, AI models change dosages dynamically to improve effectiveness while reducing negative effects.

4. Natural Language Processing (NLP) and Conversational AI.

Chatbots and virtual assistants, such as ChatGPT, Google Gemini, and Microsoft Copilot, employ RL to:

- Improve response quality based on user interactions.
- Learn unique communication techniques over time.
- Optimize sentiment analysis to detect tone and emotion.

Example: AI in Customer Support.

Amazon and Meta deploy RL-based chatbots that adjust responses based on customer behavior. These bots learn to improve client happiness by continuously upgrading their engagement tactics.

Challenges in Reinforcement Learning for Self-Improving AI.

Despite its potential, RL confronts some practical obstacles that must be addressed:

1. High Computational Costs.

RL takes tremendous computational resources to train AI agents effectively. Training deep RL models often takes weeks or months, even on high-performance GPUs.

Solution:

- Use transfer learning to apply pre-trained models instead of training from scratch.
- Implement efficient reward functions to speed up learning.

2. Exploration vs. Exploitation Dilemma.

AI must balance attempting new strategies (exploration) with sticking to existing successful strategies (exploitation). Poor balance can lead to either sluggish learning or inferior decisions.

Solution:

- Use epsilon-greedy algorithms to regulate exploration rates dynamically.
- Implement softmax action selection to introduce unpredictability while emphasizing high-reward behaviors.

3. Real-World Safety Risks.

When RL is employed in autonomous systems like self-driving cars or robotics, insufficient training can lead to dangerous or unexpected behavior.

Solution:

- Introduce safe RL techniques that minimize dangerous decisions.
- Use human-in-the-loop models to supervise early-stage learning.

Reinforcement learning is enabling AI systems to better themselves via experience, making them more adaptive and efficient. From self-driving cars that learn road conditions to trading algorithms that respond to stock market changes, RL-driven AI is already making a substantial impact.

Despite obstacles including high computing costs and unpredictability, developments in transfer learning, safe RL, and efficient training approaches are helping overcome these constraints. As RL continues to evolve, it will play a critical role in influencing the future of autonomous AI systems, intelligent robotics, and adaptive decision-making models.

3.3 Meta-Learning: AI That Learns How to Learn.

In a world where technology is growing at an unprecedented rate, AI systems must become more flexible and efficient to keep up with the pace of change. Meta-learning, sometimes referred to as "learning to learn," has emerged as one of the most inventive techniques for addressing the increasing demand for self-improving AI systems. By concentrating on how AI can increase its ability to learn from data, meta-learning helps systems to adapt quickly to new tasks, even with minimal training data. This shift towards self-optimization represents a big leap forward in AI development, with wide-ranging ramifications for industries including healthcare, robotics, finance, and natural language processing (NLP).

Meta-learning is not simply another machine learning technique; it is a paradigm change that enables machines to optimize their learning processes. Rather than relying simply on learning from static datasets, AI systems driven by meta-learning attempt to enhance their learning algorithms and generalize across diverse domains. This is particularly crucial in contexts that are dynamic or extremely uncertain, where the AI must learn quickly and adapt to unexpected conditions without needing enormous amounts of data or retraining from scratch.

In this section, we will study the fundamentals of meta-learning, how it works, its important applications, and the obstacles it faces. By analyzing how current breakthroughs in meta-learning algorithms are helping AI systems become more adaptable, we can better understand how this technique is contributing to the development of more scalable and intelligent systems.

The Concept of Meta-Learning:

- **A New Approach to Learning**.

To understand meta-learning, it's essential to think about how humans learn. When faced with a new assignment, humans don't start from scratch every time. Instead, we integrate existing knowledge obtained from similar experiences to make sense of the present situation more efficiently. For example, learning how to ride a bicycle might not be simple at first, but if we have prior experience with balance (from hobbies like skating or skiing), we might adapt faster.

In contrast, standard machine learning methods sometimes need the AI to learn everything from scratch each time a new task is introduced. This can be data-intensive and time-consuming, especially when dealing with tasks that differ greatly from those the model was originally trained on.

Meta-learning overcomes this gap by enabling machines to learn how to learn from different tasks and datasets. This strategy focuses on enhancing the learning process itself, rather than merely the outcomes of a single activity. Meta-learning algorithms find patterns and techniques that may be applied across many tasks so that when a new task occurs, the AI can apply existing knowledge or transfer learning to accelerate the learning process.

How Meta-Learning Works:

- **Key Approaches and Algorithms.**

Meta-learning comprises numerous methodologies, each concentrating on a distinct component of how AI might grow more efficient in learning tasks. The three basic paradigms of meta-learning are:

1. Model-Based Meta-Learning.

2. Optimization-Based Meta-Learning.

3. Metric-Based Meta-Learning.

Let's investigate each of these approaches in greater detail:

1. Model-Based Meta-Learning:

- **Learning Efficient Representations.**

In model-based meta-learning, the goal is to construct a model that can learn to adapt fast to new tasks by learning efficient representations of data. This strategy often incorporates neural networks that learn to analyze a task's data in a way that can be generalized to similar tasks. These models are trained in a way that they can store and reuse learned knowledge when confronted with new tasks.

- One of the essential components of model-based meta-learning is the concept of memory-augmented neural networks (MANNs). These networks are designed to retain and recall learned knowledge effectively, allowing them to adapt swiftly to new surroundings.

Example: Meta-Learning in Robotics.

In robotics, model-based meta-learning allows robots to learn how to execute various tasks, such as gripping items or assembling components. For instance, a robot might learn how to pick up a range of objects by using earlier experience from similar tasks, such as picking up objects of varied shapes and sizes. By exploiting this learned knowledge, the robot may adapt more quickly to novel tasks without having to be retrained from scratch.

- **Optimization-Based Meta-Learning:** Adapting the Learning Algorithm Itself. Optimization-based meta-learning focuses on optimizing the learning algorithm itself to make it more adaptive. This strategy often involves altering hyperparameters or the structure of the learning process, enabling the model to converge faster when meeting new problems.
- A significant method within optimization-based meta-learning is model-agnostic meta-learning (MAML), which tries to establish a set of initial parameters for a model that can quickly be adapted to new tasks with few modifications. MAML trains the model by using various tasks and applying minor updates that can be transmitted across other domains.

Example: Personalized Medicine and Healthcare.

In the healthcare industry, optimization-based meta-learning can considerably increase the performance of AI in tailored treatment. For example, AI systems can learn to swiftly adapt to new patient data, such as medical history, genetic information, or lifestyle factors. Instead of building a different model for each individual, meta-learning allows the system to swiftly respond to new cases, providing more accurate diagnoses and treatment plans without the need for extensive retraining.

3. Metric-Based Meta-Learning:

- **Learning Similarities across Tasks.** Metric-based meta-learning focuses on learning a similarity function between activities, such that the AI may generalize across tasks by recognizing similarities between them. The model is trained to quantify the distance between tasks or data points, enabling it to recognize how closely a new task is connected to ones it has already experienced.

- Siamese networks and prototypical networks are examples of algorithms used in metric-based meta-learning. These networks learn to identify tasks based on their proximity to previously encountered examples, letting AI systems make better decisions in new and unpredictable contexts.

Example: Visual Recognition Systems.

In computer vision, metric-based meta-learning can be used to improve picture identification tasks. For instance, a system taught to recognize animals in photographs can learn to generalize to new species or environmental situations. When faced with a new image classification job, the model can compare it to previously learned instances, indicating if it belongs to a given category based on the proximity to existing categories.

Applications of Meta-Learning:

- **Real-World Impact**

Meta-learning is already being implemented across numerous industries to improve efficiency, adaptability, and scalability. Below are some of the areas where this technology is having a significant impact:

1. Personalized Learning in Education.

Meta-learning holds the potential to improve education by tailoring learning experiences for each learner. AI systems can analyze how students learn best and adjust their lesson plans to maximize the learning experience for each individual. As the system encounters new students, it may change its teaching tactics based on existing knowledge from comparable students, boosting learning outcomes without requiring enormous amounts of data.

Example: AI Tutoring Systems.

Khan Academy and Duolingo are already employing AI to tailor learning for consumers. By utilizing meta-learning methodologies, these platforms can adjust to each student's learning pace, interests, and strengths, giving a more engaging and efficient educational experience.

2. Autonomous Vehicles.

Meta-learning is a vital component of the development of autonomous cars, which need to constantly adapt to changing road conditions, impediments, and driving behaviors. With meta-learning, these cars can enhance their decision-making algorithms over time by learning from past driving events and adapting to new environments without requiring extensive retraining.

Example: Tesla's Full Self-Driving System.

Tesla's Full Self-Driving (FSD) technology is powered by meta-learning algorithms that enable the car to respond to diverse driving conditions, including weather changes, road layouts, and unexpected events. This allows Tesla vehicles to enhance their performance continuously by learning from every driving experience.

3. Financial Market Prediction.

The financial market is a dynamic and complicated system that requires AI models to respond quickly to new data. Meta-learning enables AI systems to learn from prior market data, understand trends, and adapt to current market situations. By learning how to quickly alter tactics based on historical performance, AI can boost trading algorithms and portfolio management.

Example: AI in High-Frequency Trading.

High-frequency trading (HFT) firms like Two Sigma employ meta-learning to change their trading tactics based on real-time market data. This allows them to foresee trends and make timely adjustments to their investments, remaining ahead of the competition.

Challenges and Future Directions.

While meta-learning has shown significant promise, it still faces several challenges:

1. Data Efficiency.

Meta-learning seeks to eliminate the requirement for huge datasets, although it is still not totally free from data inefficiencies. Achieving optimal performance across diverse domains with insufficient data remains a challenge, particularly when tasks are drastically different from one another.

2. Computational Complexity.

Meta-learning techniques, especially those based on deep learning models, need large computer resources to train and apply. Reducing the computing cost while preserving the model's performance is an ongoing subject of research.

3. Generalization and Robustness.

While meta-learning enhances generalization, there is still work to be done in ensuring that AI systems can adapt to a wide range of tasks without overfitting to specific training data. Ensuring the durability of these systems in uncertain contexts is vital for their widespread adoption.

Chapter 4: Scalable AI Software Engineering.

4.1 Micro services and API Design for AI.

Artificial intelligence is no longer confined to research labs or theoretical conversations. It has become a key aspect of real-world applications, powering anything from chatbots and recommendation systems to autonomous vehicles and fraud detection systems. However, as AI systems become increasingly complex and data-driven, traditional monolithic designs struggle to keep up with the requirement for scalability, stability, and maintainability. This is where micro services and API-driven architectures give a strong solution.

Micro services break down huge, closely connected programs into smaller, autonomous services that communicate over APIs. This design strategy allows AI systems to scale efficiently, handle changing workloads, and connect easily with diverse platforms. Companies like Netflix, OpenAI, and Google have already utilized micro services and APIs to create high-performance AI solutions.

This chapter focuses on how micro services and APIs enable scalable AI development. It addresses the essential ideas of micro services in AI, the role of APIs, best practices for creating AI-driven micro services, and real-world applications that benefit from this approach.

Why Micro services Are Essential for AI Systems.

The emergence of AI applications has led to an increased demand for distributed computing, real-time data processing, and model deployment at scale. Traditional monolithic AI systems—where the entire program is created as a single unit—create bottlenecks in performance, making it impossible to expand or adjust certain sections of the system.

Micro services offer a solution by dividing down AI functionalities into smaller, independent services that can be created, deployed, and expanded separately.

Some significant reasons why AI-driven applications benefit from a micro services design include:

1. Scalability—AI workloads are very changeable. A micro services strategy enables separate AI components (e.g., data preprocessing, model inference, and result interpretation) to grow independently based on demand.

2. Flexibility—Developers can upgrade or replace specific services without affecting the overall system, ensuring continual improvement and faster innovation cycles.

3. Fault Isolation—If a single service fails (e.g., an image recognition module), the rest of the system remains operational. This saves downtime and enhances reliability.

4. Technology Agnosticism—each service can be constructed using the best-suited programming language and framework, enabling fast AI model deployment across varied contexts.

5. Easy Maintenance—a micro services approach makes it easy for teams to collaborate, test, and deploy AI models without interrupting the overall system.

Many large-scale AI-driven platforms, such as Spotify's recommendation system and Tesla's autonomous driving software, employ micro services to provide continuous updates and fast AI processing.

Key Components of AI Micro services Architecture.

Micro services architecture in AI development consists of numerous independent services, each handling a distinct purpose. These services operate together through well-defined APIs to create a holistic AI experience.

A typical AI micro services system includes:

1. **Data Ingestion Service**—Handles real-time or batch data collection from sources like IoT devices, APIs, or databases.

2. **Preprocessing Service**—cleans and transforms raw data in an organized manner for AI models.

3. **Model Training Service**—Trains and fine-tunes machine learning models using historical data.

4. **Inference Service**—Runs trained models on new data to provide predictions or classifications.

5. **Monitoring and Logging Service**— Tracks model performance, API calls, and system health for debugging and optimization.

6. **User Interface or API Gateway**— Provides access for external applications, mobile devices, or third-party integrations.

Each of these services can be independently deployed, scaled, and maintained without impacting other components of the AI system.

API Design for AI Micro services.

APIs (Application Programming Interfaces) are the communication layer between micro services, allowing different AI components to interact efficiently. A well-designed API enables secure, reliable, and rapid communication between micro services while preserving ease of integration.

Best Practices for API Design in AI Micro services.

1. Use RESTful or GraphQL APIs for Flexibility.

RESTful APIs are frequently utilized due to their simplicity and scalability. However, for AI-driven apps that demand personalized replies, GraphQL delivers more efficient data fetching.

Example: OpenAI's ChatGPT API leverages. REST to give text-based AI responses, whereas Spotify's recommendation API benefits from GraphQL's flexibility in obtaining user-specific preferences.

2. Asynchronous Communication for Real-Time AI Processing.

AI applications frequently require high-throughput real-time data processing. Using asynchronous APIs with message queues (e.g., Kafka, RabbitMQ) allows micro services to manage massive workloads without delays.

Example: Tesla's Autopilot technology interprets real-time sensor input asynchronously, ensuring that vehicles adapt swiftly to road conditions.

3. Versioning for Continuous Improvement.

AI models and services frequently develop. API versioning ensures that previous versions remain operational while new models get released without compromising compatibility.

Example: Google Cloud's Vision API supports many versions to allow customers to switch to newer image recognition models smoothly.

4. Security and Authentication.

AI APIs should be protected using OAuth 2.0, JWT tokens, and role-based access controls (RBAC) to prevent illegal access.

Example: Healthcare AI APIs, such as IBM Watson's medical diagnostics, implement rigorous authentication to safeguard patient data privacy.

5. Rate Limiting and Load Balancing.

To prevent excessive consumption, APIs should incorporate rate restrictions and disperse workloads using load balancers.

Example: Twitter's AI-driven sentiment analysis API imposes rate constraints to manage millions of API calls each day.

By adopting these principles, AI-driven APIs can scale efficiently while retaining performance and security.

Real-World Applications of AI Micro services and API-Driven Systems.

Several sectors have utilized AI micro services to construct scalable and adaptive AI-powered apps.

1. E-Commerce: Personalized Shopping Recommendations.

Amazon and Shopify utilize AI-driven micro services to study user behavior and deliver personalized product recommendations.

A recommendation engine microservice works autonomously, obtaining real-time purchase trends and connecting with an API that changes suggestions across web and mobile apps.

2. Autonomous Vehicles: Sensor Fusion and Decision-Making.

Tesla's Full Self-Driving (FSD) system relies on micro services that process sensor data, detect objects, and make driving decisions in real time.

Each microservice (vision processing, lane detection, object tracking) works separately but communicates over APIs to ensure safe driving decisions.

3. Healthcare: AI-Powered Diagnostics.

IBM Watson Health uses AI to evaluate medical pictures and offer treatment plans.

Micro services handle multiple duties, such as image processing, disease identification, and patient history analysis, while APIs allow hospitals to connect AI diagnostics with their electronic health record (EHR) systems.

4. Financial Services: Fraud Detection and Risk Management.

PayPal and Mastercard deploy AI-driven fraud detection micro services that evaluate millions of transactions each second.

APIs guarantee that financial institutions can query AI models in real time to identify questionable transactions without disrupting the entire banking system.

Challenges and Future of AI Micro services.

While AI micro services enable scalability and flexibility, they also present challenges:

1. Inter-Service Communication Complexity—Managing latency, data consistency, and network reliability across numerous micro services is critical.

2. Deployment and Orchestration—Kubernetes and Docker help deploy AI micro services efficiently, but configuring them for high-performance AI workloads needs knowledge.

3. Data Management and Storage—AI-driven systems need efficient data pipelines to handle large-scale data storage, retrieval, and processing.

4. Security Risks—Decentralized micro services increase attack surfaces. Secure API authentication and encryption are necessary to protect AI models and user data.

As AI systems continue to evolve, serverless AI micro services and edge AI architectures will further boost scalability by minimizing cloud dependencies and enabling real-time AI processing on IoT devices, mobile phones, and autonomous machines.

By implementing micro services and API-driven architectures, AI developers may design scalable, resilient, and high-performance AI applications capable of meeting the escalating needs of current AI-driven businesses. The future of AI development lies in breaking monolithic limitations and embracing a modular, interconnected ecosystem where AI can continuously adapt and improve.

4.2 Distributed AI Systems and Cloud-Based Adaptability.

Artificial intelligence has grown beyond standalone applications and local processing. The increasing demand for real-time inference, complex computations, and large-scale data processing has led to the rise of distributed AI systems. These systems allow AI models to operate across multiple machines, improving efficiency, scalability, and adaptability.

At the same time, cloud computing plays a crucial role in AI's evolution. Cloud platforms provide access to scalable infrastructure, on-demand resources, and real-time collaboration, making AI solutions more adaptable to different industries. Companies such as Google,

Microsoft, and Amazon have invested heavily in cloud-based AI services, enabling businesses to deploy intelligent applications without maintaining their own expensive hardware.

This chapter covers how distributed AI systems enhance scalability, the role of cloud computing in AI adaptability, and real-world examples of AI-driven cloud solutions that are shaping industries today.

Why AI Needs Distributed Systems.

Traditional AI models rely on single-machine processing, which limits computational power and slows down model training. With increasing dataset sizes and more complex deep learning architectures, AI applications require distributed computing to handle workloads efficiently.

Key benefits of distributed AI systems:

1. Faster Training and Inference—splitting training tasks across multiple GPUs or cloud instances reduces processing time.

2. Scalability—AI applications can automatically allocate additional computing resources as needed.

3. Fault Tolerance—Distributed AI allows models to continue running even if some machines fail.

4. Cost Efficiency—Cloud-based AI scales usage up or down based on demand, reducing unnecessary expenses.

5. Collaboration—AI teams across different locations can work on the same model in real time.

Industries such as self-driving cars, healthcare, and finance depend on distributed AI systems to process large amounts of data without latency issues.

Key Components of a Distributed AI System.

A distributed AI system consists of numerous components working together to complete complicated machine learning tasks. The most critical elements include:

1. Data Storage and Management.

AI applications need distributed databases such as Apache Cassandra or Google BigQuery to handle enormous volumes of organized and unstructured data.

Cloud storage solutions like AWS S3 and Google Cloud Storage ensure seamless access to datasets for AI training.

2. Parallel Processing with GPUs and TPUs.

Training deep learning models requires massive computational power. GPUs (Graphics Processing Units) and TPUs (Tensor Processing Units) distribute workloads across multiple processors for efficient training.

Example: OpenAI's ChatGPT models use thousands of NVIDIA A100 GPUs to process millions of queries per day.

3. Distributed Training Frameworks.

TensorFlow Distributed, PyTorch Distributed, and Horovod enable AI models to be trained across multiple machines.

These frameworks optimize the way AI models share calculations, minimizing redundancy.

4. Edge Computing for Real-Time AI.

Some AI applications, such as autonomous drones and smart security cameras, process data on edge devices instead of depending entirely on cloud servers.

Example: Tesla's self-driving cars process sensor data on distributed edge networks to make real-time driving decisions.

How Cloud Computing Enhances AI Adaptability.

Cloud platforms provide AI systems with scalability, flexibility, and cost-effective solutions for managing workloads. Instead of investing in on-premise AI infrastructure, businesses can deploy AI models on cloud services such as AWS, Azure, and Google Cloud AI.

1. Cloud-Based AI Infrastructure.

Cloud platforms offer:

Scalable Compute Power—AI workloads vary dynamically using Kubernetes, AWS Lambda, and Google Cloud Functions.

Pre-Trained AI Models—many cloud providers provide pre-trained models, decreasing training time.

AutoML Capabilities—Cloud-based AutoML technologies allow non-experts to construct AI applications.

Example: Google Cloud's Vertex AI provides businesses with pre-trained models for tasks like speech recognition and image classification, making AI adoption more accessible.

2. Hybrid Cloud AI.

Many firms integrate on-premise AI systems with cloud services to boost performance and data security. Hybrid cloud AI enables:

Seamless AI model deployment across private and public cloud environments

Better control over sensitive data while leveraging the cloud for AI processing

Example: Banking institutions deploy hybrid AI systems to process consumer transactions safely while leveraging cloud-based AI for fraud detection.

3. AI-as-a-Service (AIaaS).

Cloud vendors offer AIaaS solutions, allowing enterprises to adopt AI without constructing models from scratch. These services include:

Google's AutoML for automatic machine learning

AWS Rekognition for image analysis

Azure Cognitive Services for voice and language processing

Example: Retailers utilize AIaaS to study customer behavior and personalize recommendations without hiring massive AI teams.

Applications of Distributed AI and Cloud-Based Adaptability.

1. Healthcare: AI-Powered Medical Diagnosis.

IBM Watson Health processes medical records across distributed cloud infrastructures to assist doctors with diagnoses.

AI algorithms based on medical data help diagnose diseases like cancer with increased accuracy.

2. Autonomous Vehicles: Distributed Sensor Processing.

Tesla, Waymo, and Cruise use distributed AI to handle real-time sensor data for self-driving cars.

AI models run on edge devices in automobiles, while cloud AI offers over-the-air upgrades.

3. Finance: Fraud Detection with AI.

Visa and Mastercard use cloud-based AI to evaluate millions of transactions each second.

Distributed AI models detect questionable transactions in real time and inform security teams.

4. Smart Cities: AI-Driven Traffic Managemen.t

Cities like Singapore and Los Angeles deploy AI-powered traffic monitoring.

AI models use video feeds and sensor data to optimize traffic signals and reduce congestion.

Challenges in Distributed AI and Cloud-Based AI Systems.

1. Latency Issues.

Cloud-based AI demands quick data transfer, yet network delays might harm real-time applications.

Solution: Edge computing minimizes dependency on cloud servers for real-time AI inference.

2. Data Security and Compliance.

AI models rely on sensitive data, prompting concerns about privacy restrictions (GDPR, HIPAA).

Solution: Hybrid cloud architectures keep sensitive data on private servers while employing cloud AI for processing.

3. Managing Large-Scale AI Models.

AI models require continual upgrades and tweaking for peak performance.

Solution: Cloud-based MLOps (Machine Learning Operations) automates model updates and performance tracking.

4. Computational Costs.

Training large AI models on the cloud can be expensive.

Solution: Efficient AI model compression and serverless computing reduce costs without sacrificing performance.

Future of Distributed AI and Cloud Adaptability.

The next wave of AI breakthroughs will focus on boosting distributed AI efficiency and making cloud AI more accessible. Some trends impacting the future include:

Federated Learning—AI models train across multiple decentralized devices without sharing raw data, improving privacy.

Quantum AI in Cloud Computing – Companies like IBM and Google are investing in quantum AI to solve complex AI tasks faster.

Decentralized AI Networks— Blockchain-based AI models ensure transparency and security in distributed AI systems.

As AI continues to scale, distributed computing and cloud adaptability will remain at the core of building scalable, intelligent, and self-optimizing AI systems. Businesses and researchers must continue adopting cloud-based architectures to ensure that AI applications remain efficient, reliable, and cost-effective.

4.3 CI/CD for AI: Automating Deployment and Updates.

Artificial intelligence has evolved from experimental models in research labs to core business applications that demand continuous improvements. Companies deploying AI-powered systems face challenges in scaling, updating, and maintaining models in real-world environments. Unlike traditional software, AI systems require frequent retraining, tuning, and deployment without disrupting operations.

Continuous Integration (CI) and Continuous Deployment (CD) have revolutionized traditional software engineering, and now they are being applied to AI to automate model deployment, monitoring, and updates. By integrating CI/CD pipelines into AI workflows, businesses ensure their models stay relevant, efficient, and adaptable without requiring manual intervention.

This chapter explains how CI/CD practices apply to AI, the challenges of deploying AI models at scale, and real-world examples of companies automating AI updates.

Why CI/CD Matters for AI Development.

Traditional CI/CD pipelines focus on automating code testing and deployment. However, AI systems contain extra complications, like data dependencies, model versioning, and retraining cycles. A strong AI CI/CD pipeline automates these operations, guaranteeing that AI models are continuously enhanced and delivered without downtime.

Key Benefits of CI/CD for AI:

1. Faster Model Deployment—automates the transfer from model training to production, decreasing delays.

2. Improved Model Accuracy—Ensures AI models are retrained with fresh data and fine-tuned automatically.

3. Reduced Downtime - Updates AI models without impacting ongoing company operations.

4. Scalability—Supports huge AI-driven platforms handling millions of users or transactions.

5. Version Control—Tracks different AI model versions and allows rollback if a new version performs poorly.

Many industries, such as banking, healthcare, and e-commerce, depend on CI/CD pipelines to ensure their AI models remain up-to-date and efficient in real-time scenarios.

Key Components of an AI CI/CD Pipeline.

A CI/CD pipeline for AI consists of numerous steps that automate distinct parts of AI development and deployment. The following components ensure that AI models shift from development to production seamlessly:

1. Continuous Integration (CI) for AI.

CI automates the process of integrating new data, retraining models, and testing performance. Key components include:

Data Versioning—unlike traditional software, AI systems rely on ever-changing datasets. Tools like DVC (Data Version Control) and LakeFS assist in tracking dataset versions.

Automated Model Training—CI pipelines employ cloud-based AutoML frameworks to automatically retrain models when new data enters.

Validation and Unit Testing—AI models must pass accuracy and bias testing before going to deployment. Tools like TensorFlow Extended (TFX) and PyTorch Lightning automate this testing.

2. Continuous Deployment (CD) for AI.

CD streamlines AI model distribution across many environments, ensuring the latest version is always in production. Key aspects include:

- Containerization with Docker and Kubernetes—Packaging AI models in containers ensures they execute reliably across environments.
- Model Registry and Tracking— Platforms like MLflow and Amazon

SageMaker maintain AI model versions and track performance.

- Shadow Deployments and A/B Testing—New AI models are deployed alongside older versions in a controlled manner, allowing teams to compare performance before full rollout.

Challenges in Implementing CI/CD for AI.

Applying CI/CD to AI poses distinct problems compared to traditional software development. These difficulties must be addressed to guarantee AI pipelines run efficiently.

1. Managing Large and Evolving Datasets.

AI models depend on real-time data streams that change rapidly. Unlike standard CI/CD pipelines that solely handle code updates, AI CI/CD must track:

- Data drift—when new data distributions deviate from training data, resulting in deteriorated model accuracy.
- Concept drift—when real-world conditions change over time, requiring AI models to be retrained.

Solution: Implementing data versioning techniques (e.g., DVC, Pachyderm) guarantees AI models are trained on the most recent and relevant data.

2. Automating Model Testing.

Traditional software testing focuses on unit and integration tests, but AI requires:

Performance Validation—Ensuring the AI model generalizes adequately across unseen data.

Bias and Fairness Testing—AI models must be tested for bias in real-world applications (e.g., facial recognition models).

Solution: AI CI/CD pipelines include fairness evaluation tools such as IBM AI Fairness 360 to discover and minimize model biases before deployment.

3. Handling Model Versioning and Rollbacks.

Unlike traditional software, AI models can degrade after deployment owing to data shifts. Deploying a defective model can disrupt business-critical activities.

Solution: AI CI/CD pipelines hold many model versions, allowing fast rollback if a new model performs worse than the previous version. MLflow and Amazon SageMaker provide built-in model tracking capabilities.

Examples of CI/CD for AI.

1. Netflix: Automating AI-Powered Recommendations.

Netflix employs CI/CD pipelines to update its recommendation algorithm. Every day, Netflix's AI models monitor millions of user interactions and automatically retrain depending on new viewing behaviors.

How Netflix employs AI CI/CD:

- Automated data collection and preprocessing ensure training data is constantly up to date.
- Containerized AI models in Kubernetes provide quick deployment across worldwide servers.
- A/B testing with shadow deployments ensures new models outperform old ones before release.
- Netflix's CI/CD technology ensures that every customer receives tailored content recommendations without service outages.

2. Tesla: Real-Time AI Model Updates for Autonomous Driving.

Tesla's Full Self-Driving (FSD) system continuously improves through autonomous AI model changes. The company uses CI/CD to:

- Collect real-world driving data from Tesla automobiles.
- Automatically retrain AI models using Tesla's cloud-based AI platform.
- Deploy updates to Tesla automobiles over-the-air (OTA) without necessitating service visits.
- Tesla's CI/CD pipeline ensures that its autonomous driving AI grows daily, enhancing safety and efficiency with minimal human interaction.

3. Facebook (Meta): AI CI/CD for Content Moderation.

Facebook analyzes billions of posts every day, needing AI-powered moderation algorithms to detect hazardous content in real time.

How Facebook's AI CI/CD works:

- Real-time data feeds give new training instances into content moderation AI.
- CI/CD pipelines retrain models every day, assuring better accuracy in spotting misleading and hazardous content.
- Gradual deployment with rollback procedures avoids defective models from impacting users.
- Facebook's AI CI/CD solution enables quick AI changes without compromising the platform's user experience.

Best Practices for Implementing CI/CD in AI Development.

Organizations using AI-driven CI/CD pipelines should follow the following best practices:

1. Use Automated Data Pipelines— Implement solutions like Apache Airflow to automate data ingestion and preprocessing for AI models.

2. Ensure Model Monitoring and Alerts—Deploy monitoring technologies like Prometheus and Grafana to track model accuracy and detect performance decline.

3. Implement Canary Releases—Deploy AI models to a small fraction of customers before full-scale distribution.

4. Optimize for Cost and Efficiency— Use serverless AI computing to reduce unnecessary cloud costs while preserving performance.

5. Adopt MLOps Principles—Integrate DevOps approaches with AI development to speed model deployment, monitoring, and retraining.

Trends in AI CI/CD.

As AI continues to spread across industries, new themes in AI CI/CD are emerging:

Federated Learning CI/CD—AI models learn across decentralized devices without sharing sensitive data.

Edge AI Deployment Pipelines—AI models deployed at the edge (e.g., IoT devices, smart cameras) with automatic upgrades.

Self-Healing AI Pipelines—AI systems detect problems and retrain models automatically without human intervention.

Companies that invest in automated AI deployment pipelines will have a competitive advantage, ensuring their AI applications stay dependable, scalable, and always improving.

Chapter 5: Ethical and Secure AI Adaptability.

5.1 Bias Detection and Fairness in Adaptive AI.

Artificial intelligence has advanced from simple rule-based automation to highly adaptive systems capable of learning and modifying based on data. However, as AI models become more sophisticated, they also inherit biases from the data they process. Bias in AI is not merely a technological flaw—it has real-world effects, from reinforcing social disparities to making wrong or unfair decisions in crucial sectors such as healthcare, hiring, and law enforcement.

Bias detection and fairness in AI are not simply ethical considerations; they are vital for generating trust, guaranteeing legal compliance, and preserving AI's long-term survival. Addressing prejudice involves a combination of careful data selection, algorithmic transparency, constant monitoring, and human control.

Understanding Bias in AI Models.

Bias in AI develops when a model systematically favors certain outcomes or groups over others. It typically arises from one of three sources:

1. Data Bias.

AI models learn from historical data, which may represent existing socioeconomic imbalances. If the data is imbalanced—such as a facial recognition system trained largely on lighter-skinned individuals—the AI would likely perform poorly on darker-skinned faces. This issue became publicly acknowledged in 2018 after studies demonstrated that commercial facial recognition software had higher error rates for those with darker skin tones.

2. Algorithmic Bias.

Even if training data is balanced, the way an AI model analyzes and weighs information might generate bias. Some algorithms enhance gaps by favoring features that coincide with existing inequality. For example, predictive police systems based on prior crime data may erroneously target certain neighborhoods due to historical over-policing rather than actual crime rates.

3. User Interaction Bias.

AI systems that react to user behavior can unintentionally propagate biases. Social media algorithms, for instance, learn from what consumers engage with most. If inaccurate or misleading content gets more interaction, the AI may push such stuff farther, deepening echo chambers and propagating misinformation.

Methods for Detecting Bias in Adaptive AI.

To ensure fairness, AI developers must regularly monitor and audit their models for bias. Several strategies have been developed to detect and assess unfairness in AI systems.

1. Dataset Audits and Representation Analysis.

Before training an AI model, it is necessary to check the dataset for imbalances. This involves:

- Checking if specific demographics are underrepresented in training data.
- Identifying skewed distributions that may influence AI predictions.

- Using tools like IBM's AI Fairness 360 or Google's What-If Tool to examine dataset fairness.

For instance, AI-based credit scoring models have been found to prefer male applicants over female applicants, not because of deliberate gender prejudice but due to the historical financial data used to train the models. By balancing datasets and ensuring varied representation, developers can eliminate systemic prejudice.

2. Statistical Fairness Metrics.

Several mathematical techniques assist in revealing unfair bias in AI predictions. Common metrics include:

- **Disparate Impact Ratio**: Compares how different groups are treated by the AI model. If one group receives favorable outcomes at a much higher rate than another, it suggests potential bias.

- **Equalized Odds**: Ensures that AI models make equally accurate predictions across different groups.
- **Calibration Testing**: Checks whether predictions align with real-world probabilities across demographics.

For example, a healthcare AI model predicting disease risk should perform equally effectively for all ethnic groups. If it disproportionately labels particular populations as high-risk while missing cases in others, modifications are needed.

3. Counterfactual Testing

Counterfactual testing entails assessing how an AI model would behave if a critical trait (e.g., gender, race, or age) was changed while keeping everything else the same. If the model's decision changes dramatically, it suggests bias.

For instance, if an AI system suggests larger credit limits to men compared to women with comparable financial histories, it shows discriminatory decision-making.

Approaches to Reducing Bias in AI.

Detecting prejudice is merely the first step. AI developers must actively avoid biases by enhancing data quality, tweaking algorithms, and assuring openness.

1. Data Rebalancing and Augmentation.

If bias originates from unequal data representation, developers can:

- Collect more diverse training data to ensure balanced representation.

- Use synthetic data generation to create underrepresented cases.
- Apply re-weighting approaches that provide higher value to minority group samples.

For example, in 2021, researchers enhanced voice recognition systems for African American English by training models on more diverse samples. The prior systems had greater error rates since they were largely trained on Standard American English.

2. Algorithmic Fairness Adjustments.

AI models can be constructed to account for fairness directly by:

- Adding fairness requirements to prevent disproportionate consequences.
- Using adversarial debiasing, where a secondary model learns to discover and fix bias in predictions.

- Regularizing models so they do not rely too much on biased patterns in the data.

For example, hiring AI systems have been updated to omit gender-related phrases in resumes to decrease hiring prejudice.

3. Human-in-the-Loop (HITL) Oversight.

No AI system should be left totally on autopilot while making high-stakes judgments. Implementing human oversight ensures accountability by:

- Allowing manual review of AI-generated judgments as necessary.
- Using explainable AI (XAI) strategies so that humans understand why an AI model made a given decision.
- Creating bias review boards that regularly analyze AI system fairness.

Financial organizations now use human-AI hybrid decision-making to prevent biased loan approvals. AI suggests results, but human analysts evaluate fairness before completing judgments.

Legal and Ethical Implications of Bias in AI.

Governments and regulatory agencies worldwide are implementing rules and guidelines to prevent AI discrimination.

1. EU AI Act (2024).

The European Union is preparing rules to regulate AI fairness and accountability.

Companies utilizing high-risk AI (e.g., biometric identification, employment algorithms) must prove fairness and transparency.

2. U.S. AI Bill of Rights (2022).

The White House recommended standards assuring AI would not encourage bigotry.

AI systems influencing employment, finance, and healthcare must pass bias checks.

3. GDPR and AI Accountability.

The General Data Protection Regulation (GDPR) states that people have a right to comprehend AI choices that influence them.

Companies failing to address AI prejudice face lawsuits and public outrage. In 2023, a prominent social media business had to retrain its ad-serving algorithm when research revealed that job adverts for high-paying professions were presented more frequently to men than women.

The Future of Fair AI Adaptability.

Bias detection and fairness in AI are ongoing difficulties rather than one-time fixes. As AI systems grow more adaptive, they must be regularly evaluated for fairness, just like they are improved for accuracy and efficiency.

Future advancements will include:

AI ethics committees are embedded in tech businesses to examine fairness before deploying new AI technologies.

Self-correcting AI models that automatically modify when bias is identified.

Global AI fairness guidelines to maintain consistency across industries and countries.

Bias in AI is not only a technical issue; it affects human lives. The goal is to design

AI systems that serve all users equally and fairly, rather than exacerbate existing inequities.

5.2 Secure AI Development and Data Privacy.

Artificial intelligence is revolutionizing industries by automating processes, boosting decision-making, and personalizing user experiences. However, as AI systems become increasingly embedded into daily life, concerns about security and data privacy are mounting. Organizations implementing AI must prioritize secure development methods to protect sensitive data, prevent cyber risks, and maintain compliance with global legislation.

AI models rely on enormous volumes of data to learn and improve. This data often includes personal information, financial records, medical history, and private business facts. If incorrectly handled, AI technologies can become a conduit for data breaches, unlawful spying, and unethical exploitation. Secure AI development involves a balance between innovation and responsible data management.

Threats to AI Security and Data Privacy.

AI poses new dangers that standard security techniques may not fully address. These hazards originate from both external cyberattacks and internal flaws inside AI algorithms.

1. Adversarial Attacks against AI Models.

Adversarial assaults affect AI systems by adding false inputs that deceive models into making incorrect predictions. These attacks are particularly problematic for:

Facial recognition systems: Attackers can change photos significantly, making AI algorithms misidentify faces or bypass authentication procedures.

Autonomous vehicles: Small, undetectable changes to road signs can cause self-driving cars to misread traffic laws.

Spam filters and fraud detection: Attackers can alter phishing emails so that AI-powered security systems fail to detect them.

In 2023, researchers revealed how AI-powered surveillance cameras may be deceived by manipulated images, allowing individuals to skip security checks unnoticed. This type of issue underlines the need for powerful adversarial defense mechanisms in AI security.

2. Data Poisoning Risks

Data poisoning happens when attackers modify training data to induce bias or decrease AI performance. Since AI models learn patterns from prior data, polluting even a small fraction can significantly damage accuracy.

For example, if an AI-based employment system is trained on faked resumes, it may start favoring certain individuals while unfairly rejecting others. In cybersecurity, a poisoned dataset could mislead AI-driven threat detection algorithms into disregarding legitimate threats.

Tech businesses increasingly adopt strong data verification measures to prevent adversary tampering. Ensuring data integrity is a vital step in safeguarding AI development.

3. Privacy Violations in AI Training.

AI technologies, particularly large-scale deep learning models, often retain remnants of the data they were trained on. This can result in unintentional data leakage, where personal details appear in AI-generated outputs.

A serious incident occurred in 2023 when researchers found that AI language models could recall and reproduce chunks of private conversations utilized during training. This prompted worries about:

Confidential corporate data is being leaked when employing AI for document processing.

Personal information being exposed when dealing with AI-powered chatbots.

Sensitive medical records are being integrated into AI-generated answers.

To reduce these concerns, firms must implement privacy-preserving strategies, such as differential privacy and secure multi-party computation, when training AI models.

Best Practices for Secure AI Development.

Developers must integrate security measures from the outset rather than considering them as an afterthought. The following measures help ensure AI systems are resilient, reliable, and privacy-conscious.

1. Secure Model Training and Deployment.

AI models must be safeguarded throughout their lifecycle—from training and validation to deployment and continuing modifications. Secure development approaches include:

- Using encrypted datasets to prevent illegal access.
- Applying federated learning to train models on decentralized data sources without sharing sensitive information.
- Regularly assessing AI models for weaknesses that attackers might exploit.

Google and Apple now use federated learning in mobile AI systems, allowing user devices to improve AI models locally without sharing personal data with centralized servers. This drastically decreases privacy risks.

2. Implementing Differential Privacy.

Differential privacy ensures that AI models do not reveal individual data points when learning from a dataset. It works by injecting controlled noise into data, making it theoretically difficult to trace AI choices back to specific humans.

This approach is utilized in:

- Healthcare AI systems to examine patient data without revealing names.
- Financial fraud detection to improve security models without exposing user transactions.
- Smart assistants to improve voice recognition without retaining raw voice recordings.
- Tech giants like Microsoft and Meta now include differentiated privacy in their AI-powered analytics tools

to comply with data protection requirements.

3. Secure API Design for AI Services.

Many AI applications rely on APIs (Application Programming Interfaces) to communicate with other systems. However, improperly built APIs might leak critical data or allow unauthorized access.

To protect AI APIs:

- Use authentication tokens and role-based access controls to limit API usage.
- Encrypt all API calls and answers to prevent data interception.
- Monitor API traffic for strange activities that might suggest a cyberattack.
- Cloud-based AI systems now restrict API requests to approved users and

log every transaction to prevent data exploitation.

4. Explainability and Transparency in AI Decisions.

Many AI security issues occur because AI models act as black boxes, generating judgments that are difficult to comprehend. If people cannot understand why an AI system made a specific conclusion, it becomes tougher to uncover bias, manipulation, or privacy concerns.

Tech leaders push for explainable AI (XAI) techniques, including:

- Providing comprehensive documentation on how AI models make judgments.
- Using interpretable models that illustrate crucial decision criteria.
- Allowing people to argue AI-generated outcomes in sensitive applications like banking or healthcare.

- Governments are now mandating AI companies to reveal model behavior, especially in high-risk applications such as credit scoring and biometric identification.

Data Privacy Regulations Shaping AI Security.

Global policies are impacting how AI developers handle user data and model security. Companies must comply with shifting legal frameworks to avoid penalties and keep consumer trust.

1. General Data Protection Regulation (GDPR).

The European Union's GDPR establishes severe limits on AI data usage, including:

The right to be forgotten, allowing people to request AI systems remove their data.

Explicit user consent before collecting or processing personal information.

Severe fines for data breaches, driving corporations to upgrade security procedures.

Under GDPR, AI-driven chatbots and virtual assistants must inform users how their data is processed and stored.

2. U.S. AI and Data Protection Laws.

The United States has introduced many AI security policies, including:

The AI Risk Management Framework (NIST 2023), which gives advice for secure AI implementation.

The AI Bill of Rights (2022) ensures AI does not hurt consumers through biased or opaque decision-making.

Major financial institutions now examine their AI systems to line with these standards and prevent liability issues.

3. China's AI Security Regulations.

China has developed severe AI policies, requiring:

AI-generated content will be explicitly labeled to prevent misleading.

AI businesses are to undergo security audits before introducing new models.

Stringent data storage restrictions, limiting cross-border data exchanges.

AI enterprises operating in China must demonstrate security compliance before deploying AI-powered products.

The Secure of AI and Privacy-First Development.

Security and privacy are becoming essential factors in AI research. As AI systems continue to evolve, firms must:

Adopt privacy-enhancing technologies (PETs) to protect user data.

Develop self-healing AI models that detect and respond to security risks in real-time.

Align AI security initiatives with global compliance laws to generate customer trust.

Leading enterprises are now implementing privacy-first AI frameworks into their systems, ensuring AI-powered solutions stay secure, ethical, and resilient against cyber threats.

5.3 AI Governance and Regulatory Compliance.

Artificial intelligence has evolved beyond research labs and is now firmly integrated into businesses such as finance, healthcare, and national security. This rapid adoption brings substantial ethical and legal implications. AI governance and regulatory compliance ensure that AI systems stay safe, fair, and accountable. Without clear norms, corporations face legal penalties, reputational loss, and detrimental societal effects.

The Need for AI Governance.

AI governance is not simply about following laws—it is about building AI systems that match with human ideals. The necessity for governance has risen owing to real-world events where AI has been misused or has led to unanticipated effects.

One example is facial recognition technology. Governments and organizations have adopted it for security and identity, but it has also created severe privacy concerns. Studies have demonstrated that some facial recognition algorithms misidentify members of specific ethnic groups at higher rates than others. This has led to false arrests and security threats. In response, some governments have prohibited the use of face recognition in public settings, while others are working on stronger rules to limit its implementation.

Another example is AI-powered hiring tools. Many firms utilize machine learning models to screen job applications; however, some of these algorithms have been discovered to be biased. If an AI model is trained on historical employment data that favored specific demographics, it can unintentionally bias against equally qualified candidates from underrepresented groups. Without effective control, corporations could risk litigation and public criticism.

Key Pillars of AI Governance.

Governance frameworks differ across industries and geographies, but several key ideas remain consistent:

1. Transparency and Explainability.

AI systems should not operate as "black boxes." Businesses must ensure that their models provide reasons for their actions. This is especially critical in sectors like healthcare and finance, where AI-driven suggestions can touch lives. For example, if a bank declines a loan application based on an AI decision, the applicant should have the right to understand why.

Explainability is also vital for troubleshooting and developing AI models. Companies that invest in interpretable AI systems can immediately discover biases or errors before they cause harm. Tools like SHAP (Shapley Additive Explanations) and LIME (Local Interpretable Model-Agnostic Explanations) assist data scientists in comprehending how AI algorithms make decisions.

2. Accountability and Human Oversight.

AI should not replace human judgment but instead operate alongside it. Organizations must develop explicit responsibility systems for AI-related choices. This implies identifying who is responsible when an AI system makes a mistake.

For example, with autonomous vehicles, if an AI-driven automobile causes an accident, who should be held accountable—the manufacturer, the software developer, or the car owner? Companies like Tesla and Waymo have faced criticism over similar vulnerabilities. Regulations are now being established to ensure that duty is properly assigned.

Human oversight is also important in high-risk AI applications. In medicine, AI models assist doctors in detecting disorders, although final choices should always be evaluated by medical professionals. This protects AI from making potentially fatal errors.

3. Fairness and Bias Mitigation.

Bias in AI is a big worry, and governance frameworks must handle it.

Organizations should undertake bias audits on their AI models and employ diverse datasets to train their systems. Governments and industry groups are asking for uniform fairness testing to ensure AI does not discriminate.

For example, amid public pressure, prominent tech companies had to update their AI algorithms to remove racial and gender prejudices in their products. Some organizations now engage AI ethics teams to assess their models before deployment.

4. Security and Data Protection.

AI models rely on enormous volumes of data, making them ideal targets for hackers. Without sufficient security measures, AI systems can be controlled, leading to fraud or misinformation.

Deepfake technology is a good example of how AI may be exploited. AI-generated deepfakes have been used to manufacture fake news, mimic public personalities, and influence stock markets. To prevent this, firms and regulators are creating watermarking techniques and detection technologies to identify AI-generated content.

Governments are also imposing stronger data privacy rules. The European Union's General Data Protection Regulation (GDPR) and the California Consumer Privacy Act (CCPA) compel corporations to educate users about how their data is utilized in AI models. Violations might result in huge fines.

Regulatory Landscape for AI.

Countries and international entities are rapidly working to control AI. While there is no uniform AI legislation, numerous nations have created regulations to guide ethical AI development.

United States.

- The U.S. has developed a sector-specific approach to AI regulation. For example:
- The FDA (Food and Drug Administration) regulates AI in medical devices.
- The SEC (Securities and Exchange Commission) oversees AI-driven trading systems.
- The Federal Trade Commission (FTC) has warned corporations

against employing biased AI in hiring and financing.

- The Biden administration has also suggested an AI Bill of Rights, establishing standards for safe and fair AI use.

European Union.

The EU AI Act is one of the most extensive AI regulatory ideas. It classifies AI applications into distinct danger levels:

- **Unacceptable risk**: AI systems that harm human rights (e.g., mass surveillance) will be banned.
- **High risk:** AI in healthcare, law enforcement, and essential infrastructure must meet tight restrictions.
- **Limited risk:** Chatbots and recommendation systems must be transparent but face fewer restrictions.

The EU AI Act is expected to set a global standard, similar to how GDPR influenced data privacy laws worldwide.

China.

China has taken an aggressive stance on AI regulation. The government has introduced rules for AI recommendation algorithms, requiring platforms like TikTok to provide users with the option to disable algorithm-driven content. China also mandates security reviews for AI systems that influence public opinion.

Other Countries

Canada is working on the Artificial Intelligence and Data Act (AIDA) to govern AI in business applications.

India is drafting policies for AI in financial services and healthcare.

Brazil has introduced AI ethical rules, focused on transparency and accountability.

Corporate AI Governance Strategies.

Leading tech businesses are adopting their own AI governance frameworks. These techniques help them comply with regulations and earn public trust.

Google's AI Principles.

Google has committed to AI principles that prioritize fairness, accountability, and social benefit. The corporation has also developed an AI ethics board to examine its projects.

Microsoft's Responsible AI Initiative.

Microsoft has embedded AI fairness and security tools into its products. It has also committed not to sell facial recognition technology to police departments due to privacy concerns.

IBM's AI Ethics Pledge.

IBM has developed open-source technologies for AI bias detection. The corporation is also advocating for government-industry cooperation to produce common AI ethics guidelines.

Challenges in AI Governance.

Despite advancements, AI governance still confronts difficulties.

1. Regulations Struggle to Keep Up.

AI technology evolves faster than rules can be written. Governments typically struggle to govern developing AI applications, such as generative AI models like ChatGPT and DALL•E.

2. Global Coordination Is Lacking.

Distinct countries have distinct AI policies, resulting in regulatory fragmentation. A corporation operating in various locations must comply with conflicting rules. International collaboration is essential to build universal AI standards.

3. Corporate Resistance.

Some corporations fight rigorous AI restrictions, fearing that they could impede innovation. Striking a balance between regulation and technological innovation remains a challenge.

The Future of AI Governance.

As AI gets more powerful, governance frameworks will need to develop. Experts believe that future rules will focus on:

Real-time AI auditing can detect biases and errors automatically.

Stronger AI security protocols to prevent cyberattacks.

Ethical AI certifications that organizations must achieve before deploying AI products.

Governments, businesses, and researchers must work together to guarantee AI serves humanity in a fair, transparent, and safe manner. AI governance is not simply about laws—it is about designing a future where AI helps all.

Conclusion.

The Future of Adaptive AI Systems.

Artificial intelligence has matured from a theoretical concept into a transformational force impacting industries, economies, and daily life. The journey toward scalable, intelligent, and self-optimizing AI is not just about technology innovation but about how systems interact with the world, adapt to new obstacles, and augment human decision-making. As AI systems continue to evolve, the responsibilities of developers, businesses, and policymakers become more crucial than ever.

Building AI That Adapts to Real-World Challenges.

The demand for AI systems that respond flexibly to new data, fluctuating market conditions, and unforeseen occurrences has never been higher. Businesses leveraging AI must ensure their systems stay adaptable and capable of handling unpredictability. The COVID-19 pandemic revealed how vital flexible AI models are. Supply chain algorithms had to be retrained to account for shortages and delivery delays, while healthcare AI had to process rapidly changing medical data to assist in diagnosing the virus.

A static AI system fails when real-world conditions vary. This is why adaptive AI frameworks that continuously update, enhance, and self-correct are becoming the standard rather than an exception. Companies that invest in self-learning AI, reinforcement learning models, and meta-learning methodologies place themselves ahead of competitors.

The Shift toward Decentralized AI.

Cloud computing has facilitated the mass deployment of AI, but the next phase is about decentralization. Edge AI—where processing happens on local devices rather than centralized servers—is gaining pace. With smart devices, autonomous vehicles, and industrial IoT applications increasing, AI models must process data in real time without relying on cloud connectivity.

Self-optimizing AI deployed at the edge is already being used in industries, where predictive maintenance algorithms assess machinery data on-site, preventing costly breakdowns. The same principle applies to autonomous drones employed in disaster relief missions, when AI systems must make split-second judgments without depending on a distant server.

The problem for engineers is ensuring these decentralized AI models remain secure and continuously improve while maintaining privacy standards. Federated learning is one way that allows models to train on decentralized data sources while protecting privacy, a concept already deployed in mobile AI applications such as Google's predictive text and Apple's Face ID updates.

Ethics, Governance, and the Future of AI Regulation.

As AI systems become more integrated into high-stakes decision-making, the subject of responsibility becomes unavoidable. The conversation around AI governance is no longer theoretical—it has real-world implications. Social media recommendation algorithms have been accused of amplifying misinformation, facial recognition has led to wrongful arrests, and hiring algorithms have shown bias against underrepresented groups.

Regulatory bodies worldwide are racing to create AI laws that balance innovation with ethical considerations. The European Union's AI Act aspires to categorize AI systems depending on their risk level, defining worldwide rules for transparency and responsibility. Meanwhile, the U.S. has adopted AI-related policies in finance, healthcare, and law enforcement to minimize bias and misuse.

For corporations and developers, compliance with AI regulations will no longer be optional. Companies failing to design transparent, fair, and explainable AI systems will suffer legal and reputational consequences. Ethical AI is not only about respecting laws—it is about ensuring AI supports humanity without unintentional harm.

AI's Role in Enhancing Human Potential.

There is a misperception that AI would replace human occupations at an unmanageable rate. While automation is transforming sectors, AI's greatest potential rests in boosting human capabilities rather than destroying them. AI-powered aides in medical research help clinicians diagnose ailments faster. AI-driven legal tools help lawyers to filter through enormous amounts of case law efficiently. Creative AI tools enable designers, artists, and authors to enhance their work rather than replace their skills.

Businesses that adopt AI as a tool for collaboration rather than substitution will gain the most. AI systems that adapt to human behavior, preferences, and processes provide greater value than those built to operate in isolation. The future is not about AI versus humans—it is about AI working with humans.

Preparing for the Next Wave of AI Breakthroughs

The fast breakthroughs in AI technology show no signs of slowing down. Generative AI models, such as ChatGPT and DALL•E, have previously exhibited the ability to create human-like text and graphics. The next wave will deliver far more advanced AI that can autonomously develop code, replicate real-world physics for scientific research, and even generate individualized education programs tailored to individual learning styles.

AI is also evolving toward self-improving systems—models that not only learn from data but also alter their own architecture, optimizing themselves for increased efficiency. This change will lead to AI systems that require less human involvement, making automation even more seamless.

At the same time, quantum computing is on the horizon. AI algorithms that presently take days to train might be refined in seconds with quantum processors, unlocking capabilities that were previously deemed unachievable. The industries that prepare for this transformation will be the first to exploit its power.

AI as a Continuous Journey.

Artificial intelligence is not a one-time solution—it is a continual process of improvement, adaptation, and responsible implementation. Companies that win in AI will be those who embrace adaptability, incorporate governance frameworks, and promote human-centered AI design.

The road ahead is packed with hurdles, from technical scalability to ethical problems. However, the potential of AI to solve complex issues, promote innovation, and enhance lives is stronger than ever. The obligation resides in ensuring AI is created for robustness, justice, and long-term effect.

AI is not simply about making smarter machines. It is about developing a wiser future.

www.ingramcontent.com/pod-product-compliance
Lightning Source LLC
LaVergne TN
LVHW041208050326
832903LV00021B/531